Heaven Exists

NOELLE McNEIL

Heaven Exists

Outskirts Press, Inc.
Denver, Colorado

Outskirts Press, Inc.
http://www.outskirtspress.com

ISBN: 978-1-4327-4102-0

Library of Congress Control Number: 2009932821

Outskirts Press and the "OP" logo are trademarks belonging to Outskirts Press, Inc.

PRINTED IN THE UNITED STATES OF AMERICA

To my family, which reached into the abyss, grabbed hold of my body and spirit, and would not let go until I was freed.

To all those who doubt, I tell you believe: heaven exists. I know; I was there.

Contents

Introduction

My name is Noelle McNeil. I am a twenty-four-year-old woman who suffered a severe, traumatic brain injury at the age of twenty. The recovery that followed has been the most important time of my life. Part of this book I wrote while still fairly early in my recovery; some I wrote recently. It is part journal, and part an accounting of my recollections and reflections.

On August 1, 2005, I was a typical college student. I had completed my sophomore year at James Madison University in Virginia and I was looking forward to returning to school. I was dating a gorgeous young man I believed to be the love of my life; I was tall, blonde, and talking to a modeling agency. Life was good. I was pursuing the activity I enjoyed most in life: competitive horseback riding. I was good at it, and had achieved national ranking. It had been another carefree summer at the Jersey Shore where I live, full of sparkling days at the beach and many hours riding at the barn. In between, there were nights partying with my friends. I was exactly where I wanted to be at that point in time. It never occurred to me that my life could change so drastically in a matter of seconds, but it did. This is my story.

1

The Journey Begins

On August 2, 2005, I began a journey that I did not plan. It has taken me to a place that I read about in Catholic school—heaven—and to a world that I only observed before from afar: the world of the disabled. Both of these occurrences have altered my life.

The accident happened at a farm in New Jersey. I was competing in a local horse show to prepare for a major horse show in Virginia the following week. I was scheduled to compete in Virginia the following week. I was to ride for the James Madison University equestrian team. This was supposed to be an ordinary horse show. It turned out to be anything but.

I have no recollection of the accident. The witnesses said that the horse I was riding refused at the jump and began to buck rear and generally go berserk in his efforts to get me off his back. Unfortunately, he was successful. I hit the ground with tremendous force. The fall rendered me unconscious immediately and broke the entire inside rim of my helmet. The helmet, the same worn by Olympic riders, was the most expensive that money can buy.

I was unresponsive at the scene; my pulse was undetectable by the laypeople there. The paramedics arrived very shortly I am told and were able to detect only a "thready" pulse, which means you are barely alive and your heart is not working very well. They called for a helicopter to transport me to the trauma center. The first of many seemingly random occurrences that enabled me to survive happened when they called for the helicopter. It was only seven minutes away, instead of the typical twenty-five minutes from their base. I was dying; twenty minutes can mean life or death in these situations.

I am told that those paramedics had to work hard to keep me alive on the way to the hospital. I was in a coma when I arrived there and remained in a coma for several weeks. I had sustained a diffuse axonal injury (DAI) as a result of the fall. Axonal injuries occur when the brain gets knocked about within the skull. It is a closed-head injury. That's when there is forward motion that is suddenly and forcefully stopped. My body stopped moving when I hit the ground, but my brain did not. It went back and forth hitting the bony ridges of the inside of my skull, which caused damage to the neurons within. They were stretched and sheared, preventing them from sending any messages.

Your brain controls virtually everything you do, so if it is disrupted it is a very serious matter. In my case everything was disrupted: my heart rate, my breathing, my consciousness. I was lost in this morass of tangled neurons, and descended into an abyss from which it is almost impossible to emerge. The prognosis for DAI injuries is horrifying, and almost invariably is the cause of significant, life changing disability in those who sustain it. Only 3 percent of people with this injury make any recovery at all. Most remain vegetative for the rest of their lives and require nursing-home care. Only 1 percent makes a significant recovery. I am part of that 1 percent.

I was sent to the intensive care unit of the Robert Wood Johnson University Hospital in New Brunswick, New Jersey, which is a regional trauma center. The staff there had their work cut out for them to keep me alive. They were up to the task. I was labeled vegetative. What a horrible thing to call a human being. My mom told the doctors they were never to call me that again and they should rewrite the books if that was the best label they could come up with. The only shred of good news at that point was that my eyes still reacted to light. My family clung to that shred of hope for dear life.

I hovered at death's door for two weeks. I developed a terrible pneumonia that almost killed me. I developed a systemic sepsis infection. My heart rate alternately raced and plummeted, and my oxygen saturation rate also dropped precipitously. The monitors crashed and my death was imminent several times, but I survived.

During the time that I hovered near death in the netherworld of coma I had a life-changing experience, one that I will never forget. One of the times I almost died, I found myself ascending through white fluffy clouds into the blue sky. It was a beautiful and peaceful experience. Once I got through the clouds I found myself walking—more accurately, gliding—over the clouds toward a very brightly lit place. I was compelled to go toward this light, and I was happy to do so. As I got closer to my destination, I was greeted by my deceased Uncle Joe, my father's brother who had died prematurely a few years earlier.

I could see through Uncle Joe, but his facial features were distinct, and I instantly recognized him. He said, "Noelle, your father is going to be upset; he did not expect you to be here so soon." I said, "Does this mean I am dead?" He responded affirmatively. There was communication between us but he was not moving his lips, nor was I. It was telepathic or spiritual communication. Uncle Joe was in front of the brightly lit place. I felt that Jesus was inside of it.

I asked Joe if this was heaven. He said "yes." I asked if I could go back because I did not want to leave my life yet; I had so much left that I wanted to do. Uncle Joe said he would ask. I didn't ask whom he was asking; I assumed it was Jesus. After what seemed to be a little while he told me I could go back. He said that I would recover but it would take a long time. The last thing Uncle Joe communicated was, "Say hi to your father for me." I said I would.

With that, I began to descend back down through the clouds. I reentered my body and the world of the living. I had been to heaven and now I would get a glimpse of what hell is: waking up to find my self totally debilitated in a hospital unable to, eat, walk, or function in any real sense. Thus began the most terrifying and difficult journey of my life, and for certain the most important one: the journey to find Noelle again. I was lost in a labyrinth of broken axons and a battered body. I would, however, be reborn.

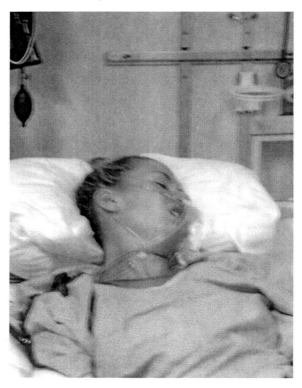

2

Reemerging

It is important to note that a person who has sustained a severe brain injury is not capable of lying or making up an elaborate story of any kind. There is a condition called disinhibition, which occurs with brain injuries of serious magnitude. Disinhibition means that you say the truth no matter what the consequence. There is no guile in a brain-injured person. Lying is actually a social skill that we all learn to survive. When I started to emerge and very matter of factly related my experience of dying and going to heaven, my family knew that I was telling the truth. The staff couldn't dispute my story; none of them had almost died and lived to tell about it. They were amazed by it. My family told me that in the first few days they would rejoice that my pupils still reacted to the flashlight that the doctors kept shining in my eyes. I lay totally still and unresponsive.

When I look at the pictures of myself in the coma I look like I am uncomfortable. I had several broken ribs and some bruising in addition to the closed-head injury. The doctors and the nurses had to keep forcing a suction tube down my throat into my lungs to extricate the thick green mucous that eventually almost killed me. I had to have a chest tube inserted to re-inflate my collapsed lung. My brother Sean told me that when they told my mom I had to have the chest tube her knees buckled.

She had been awake in the hospital with me for days. The chest tube was just too much. In addition, I had a feeding tube that went down through my nose into my stomach. I was on all sorts of monitors.

Eventually, the doctors and nurses noticed that when my family members spoke to me, my heart rate would change. My mom, dad, and Sean all believed that at some level I recognized their voices. The doctors and nurses started allowing my mom to stay in the room when they were shoving the suction tube down my throat because they felt that my heart rate stayed more stable if she spoke to me during and after they did it. Apparently it hurts to have the procedure, yet without it I surely would have suffocated. Eventually I had to have a feeding tube inserted directly into my stomach, as it was clear to the medical staff that I could not swallow, and was still comatose.

The chief trauma surgeon did the procedure. He came into my room after the surgery at eleven o'clock at night and very animatedly told my parents that he thought that I tried to say something to him. He thought I said, "I want to go home." These doctors don't lie, they tell it like is; they have to. He was elated, and so was my family. The staff at Robert Wood Johnson worked very hard to keep me alive. They gave me the opportunity to recover. I am eternally grateful to them.

After two weeks at Robert Wood Johnson, I was transferred to a brain trauma rehabilitation hospital, JFK Medical Center in Edison, New Jersey. I was placed in their intensive care brain trauma unit (BTU). JFK has an incredible reputation for brain trauma recovery. They earned it. They pretty much wrote the book on how to get people out of a coma and rehabilitate them. And they took excellent care of me.

My doctor, Dr. Malone, wanted to try a drug called amantidine. Amantidine is an antiviral drug that had the secondary effect of helping comatose people "wake up" in some cases. I was not waking up on my own. Two weeks in the hospital and I was still out of it most of the time. There were some risks associated with the drug, but they only affected a small percentage of the folks who took it.

We tried it. Someone from my family was with me twenty-four hours a day for those first few weeks. They continued to talk to me, sing to me, and touch me. They also kept moving my legs and arms so they would not totally atrophy. The doctors were very concerned that I was "gone" and would not reawaken. My mother kept telling them I was "in there" and the task was to get me out. My family never gave up hope that I would awaken. Never underestimate the value of your family and true friends. Thousands of people were praying for me. I had an ecumenical following. There were rabbis in New York City and their flock praying for me; the West Point community, where my cousin was assigned, was praying for me; Baptists, Protestants, Catholics, you name it. I was on multiple prayer lists all over the country. The Lord was being petitioned daily. My mom and her friend Debbie Williams were saying particular prayers to St. Theresa. My mom's confirmation name was Theresa after this saint; Mom's friend was a believer in devotion to St. Theresa, who is noted for miracles.

One of the things I have discovered since this injury is often things that appear to be random occurrences or coincidence are not. For instance, St. Theresa's favorite flower was the yellow rose, and she is often depicted with this flower. At the Brain Trauma Unit of JFK, as in any intensive care unit, flowers are not permitted. The scent, the space they take up, etc., just doesn't allow for it. Several floral arrangements had been sent to the hospital for me that had to be sent back. The day after my mom's friend said that she was making novenas to St. Theresa for me, a bouquet of flowers appeared in my room. They were from my grandmother, and they included three yellow roses. My room at the time was accessible from the back stairs of the hospital. This entry was not well known. Somehow the roses got through accidentally; they never would have made it past the front desk.

This was also the day when I suddenly began to speak, thirty-six hours after taking the amantidine. Coincidence? I don't think so. God gave us the gifts of faith, hope and love, and love is the greatest gift of all. The love of my family and friends sustained me through the darkest days, and there were many of them.

Emerging from a coma is not as it is depicted on television. You do not suddenly wake up and ask for ice cream. If a person has been in a coma for more the thirty-six hours, they usually have a gradual awakening that takes place over a period of days and weeks. If the brain injury is severe enough, as mine was, there is a gradual relearning of virtually everything that has to take place in order to regain function. The body weakens and atrophies from inactivity, so the simplest things such as walking, swallowing, and speaking become monumental tasks requiring months of physical, cognitive, and occupational therapy to achieve. Some never emerge from the coma; they are medically labeled vegetative or minimally conscious. In the hospital, I was housed with young people who were injured within days of my accident. Many of them remain there to this day. They are frozen in time, and prisoners of their failed bodies. God help them and their families. When I start feeling sorry for myself, I think of them, pick myself up, and move on.

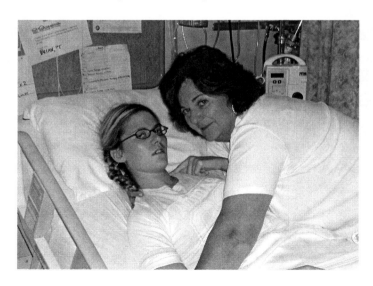

3

Telling It Like It is, and Getting Away with it

My brother's favorite memory of the brain trauma unit is the guy who kept swearing at everyone. He probably injured his frontal lobe, which controls inhibitions. He no longer had any. He was really smart though; just injured. While my family waited in the hall to see me, while the nurses were working on me they would hear this disembodied male voice yelling from his room, "Hey, who is out there? I need a nurse." The nurse would go in and he would proceed to tell her she was "f—ing useless." Then the doctor would go in and try to calm him down and he would say, "Are you done yet? Good; now you can get your sorry ass out of here because you are f—ing useless too!" Then he would spell useless for added emphasis: "U-c-e-l-e-s-s." Such are the nuances of brain trauma.

My family would be sick from laughing, and the same guy would yell, "I hear you assholes laughing out there." This of course made them laugh more. There were some good times to be had at the brain trauma unit. Sean laughs till he cries at the mere memory of it. My family is definitely a little left of center.

October 2005

The process of rehabilitation from a diffuse axonal injury is a long and arduous one. There are psychological as well as physical issues.

HEAVEN EXISTS

I had to stop taking the amantidine for a while, because it elevated my liver enzymes. During this period, I stopped talking as much as I was while on the drug. After a few days the doctors decided to try it again. The drug appeared to have a positive effect on my awareness, and my enzymes stayed stable. Everyone was overjoyed. The doctors later admitted they were concerned that I would never wake up.

Waking up was the goal, but it too came with a price tag. I remember distinctly one day at the brain trauma unit in JFK Hospital looking down and finally realizing that there was a foul-looking plastic tube protruding directly out of my abdomen. I had been vaguely aware of this, but due to the injury it hadn't fully registered until this one day. The nurses poured a liquid supplement into this tube three times a day to keep me alive. This tube was held in place by stitches. I felt like an alien. Who was this broken girl in the wheelchair, with the feeding tube? Surely this could not be me. I was entombed in a broken body from which there was no escape. I was horrified when I understood the full impact of this tube. I could not swallow food. I also became aware at this time that I was in a hospital and could not walk. My head shook from the tremors cased by the brain injury and my right hand shook uncontrollably. I emerged enough to experience the horror of being totally debilitated, in a wheelchair, wearing diapers, in a hospital with a feeding tube sticking out of my stomach. I believed that this was the way I would be for the rest of my life, totally dependent, hospital bound, destroyed; forever. I thought of Christopher Reeves. I began to ask my mother for two cyanide pills. She asked me why I wanted them; I told her that I wanted to die. I asked the staff at JFK, really anyone who would listen, to get me two cyanide pills so I could die. They wouldn't, of course, so I started wheeling my wheelchair around in efforts to find cleaning materials. I asked for Windex and Clorox; I knew if I drank them they would kill me. The irony was that I was too disabled even to kill myself; I needed help to do it. Fortunately no one was willing to help me destroy myself.

On the contrary, everyone was totally committed to helping me recover. My family promised me that I would be rid of the feeding tube, and that I would walk no matter what anyone else said. They also promised me that I would go home. The hospital had me on twenty-four-hour-a-day suicide watch for a few days, and I saw a psychiatrist. If I gave up I knew that I was done, doomed to remain totally debilitated. I prayed to God for strength. He complied.

I decided once again to choose life. God had saved me for a reason; I had asked to return to life and now the task was to muster every bit of will and to use every grace from God to get out of the wheelchair and off the feeding tube so that I could return to my home and my life. I knew that I had a destiny to fulfill. The task was to find it.

My mom suggested that I write a book about my experience. I started to write in a journal form following my release from inpatient hospitalization. My writing improves over the course of the journal as my brain healed. Afterward, I then went on to write the rest of the book. In all, I was hospitalized for a total of four and a half months, and in a wheelchair for eight and a half months. I had to use an Alpha Smart assisted technology device to write, as I can no longer write with my right hand.

4

Breaking through the Wall

Athletes know about breaking through the wall. It means going beyond your personal best and raising the bar, whatever the bar is for that person. I have been competitive my whole life. I always sought to improve my personal best. Breaking the wall was second nature to me. Well, with this injury, breaking through the wall meant learning how to walk again. The wall in this case was my injured brain. Balance is controlled by the brain. My balance center was damaged. This was to be the biggest, strongest wall imaginable. I had to break through it.

Some well-intentioned professionals informed me and my parents that I would probably not walk normally again. Their goal was to help me become a "household ambulator." Basically, that means I might be able to walk around a bit in the safety of my handicapped-accessible home, but require a wheelchair anywhere else. I am not faulting them; the level of my injury usually precludes walking. I, however, was not going to be one of the typical statistics if I could help it. My mother politely but firmly advised them that as long as my spine was not severed, if I could walk at all, I would eventually not require the wheelchair. I am sure they thought she was in denial. Thus began my twenty-four-hour-a-day rehab. I was in the best facility, JFK Medical Center's brain trauma unit, and I had the most dedicated family and friends imaginable. When the professional staff finished working on me for the day, my family started.

Weekends were particularly busy for my family pseudo-therapists, as the physical therapy staff was off. My family insisted on being trained on how to move my limbs so that I would not atrophy over the weekend. The staff complied. One of the stages of recovery from a severe brain-trauma injury is the biting phase. I went through this. I tried to bite everyone who came near me. How bizarre. I bit my family, my therapists, anybody. Maybe I was just half starving from being on the feeding tube and not being allowed to chew anything. I don't know. Eventually I stopped this behavior, much to the relief of my family and the staff. The brain is an amazing thing.

After two months in JFK I was transferred to Hartwyck at Oak Tree, a rehabilitation facility. My new doctor was Dr. Caroline McCagg, a renowned specialist in brain-trauma rehabilitation. I came to view her as a friend as well. I was so weak from months in bed that I could not stand unaided. I only weighed 121 pounds; I lost twenty pounds during the first few weeks after my accident while hospitalized. My legs looked like toothpicks. It was horrifying. My mother watched the physical therapists as they helped me stand and placed a chair behind me in case I fell. She began doing this clandestinely in my room after hours.

At first I could only stand in between her knees for support for fifteen seconds. We timed it by watching the large clock on the wall in my room. By the end of that first session I could stand for thirty seconds. I was euphoric. These sessions continued every day, and by the end of the week my physical therapist noted how much stronger I was. Eventually I got to the point where I could stand for a minute, then two minutes, and so on. My father and brother came in the room the third night when I was standing and I did so for ninety seconds, they both cried with joy. My right leg shook like crazy, but I stood.

We didn't have to do the exercises secretly anymore. The staff recognized that I was getting better much faster than anyone else was. I desperately wanted to go home from rehab. My family told me that when I could walk a bit they would take me home. My father was the leg-lift Nazi. He watched the physical therapists and supervised the same exercises in my room at night. Tom, my stepfather, helped mom move me when he came too. It was a combined effort. My mom and Tom would walk me around the parking lot of Hartwyck. We would go over and see the ducks in the pond at the end of the driveway. They had to hold onto me very firmly. I could not support myself, but I was up, on my own two feet, and moving, and that was literally a step in the right direction.

I absolutely loved seeing those ducks! Just to be outside, in the air, away from my institution was a joy. Those early sessions gave me hope that one day I would actually be free again.

My physical therapist understood me; she understood that I had always been an athlete. She understood my drive. I told her my goal was to run again. She said we would work toward that goal. Other team members thought that I was doing too much. My therapist let me go as far as I could, allowing for my individual needs. I kept asking to try the treadmill. They hooked me up to a harness so that I would not fall, and the physical therapist stood behind me on the runners. I walked alone on the treadmill for two minutes. My God I did it. My family cried as they watched. The wall now had a crack in it. I now knew that I would eventually shatter the wall.

HEAVEN EXISTS

October 30, 2005

I was always one to celebrate Halloween. I think it is a fun holiday. This year I was still hospitalized at Hartwyck. It was going to be a very different Halloween. Goosey Night rolled around, the day before Halloween, also called mischief night, when people play pranks. I started the day with the usual shower, physical therapy, occupational therapy, awful food, and then I decided to try to shave my legs. I hadn't done that in three months. My mom took care of those details. So I began by spraying shaving cream all over my legs. I then attempted to shave my legs. There was a problem however; I had sprayed the shaving cream over my jeans, and the razor didn't work too well on denim!

This type of error is common with people with a severe brain injury. Once the brain starts to remember things they are often jumbled. I finally realized what I had done and knew I could not undress myself, so I proceeded to spray the shaving cream all over the room. It was the most fun I had since this damn injury. The staff came down eventually and cleaned me up, but I was on a roll now. My room was at the end of the long hallway right by one of the exit doors. I decided to make a break for it. I wheeled myself out to the door and proceeded to push it open. The alarms went off! The next thing I saw was a bunch of staff running down the hall checking the door. They were trying to figure out who had escaped. They didn't suspect me of anything because they thought I was still too disabled to perform this action. They were wrong. So, in the middle of all this chaos I wheeled myself down to the other exit door and tried to get out that one. The alarms went off again. By now there were policemen arriving, a result of this attempted jailbreak, the alarms were going off, and the fire truck was being dispatched. What a riot, I thought, something exciting is finally happening at Hartwyck.

BREAKING THROUGH THE WALL

This time, however, they caught me in the act. I didn't know that if the alarms went off the police and the firemen had to come; I was just trying to go home. The staff was amazed that I pulled all of this off. Some of them were not too happy. The social worker Tony couldn't help but laugh. He chastised me but said, "We want you to go home too, but not just yet." They called my mom and summoned her to Hartwyck, to report my bad behavior. She came and asked me what the hell I thought I was doing. I explained that it was mischief night and that I was being mischievous! Mom started laughing. The staff was looking for her to be duly ashamed of my actions. She told them that she was happy that I knew what day it was, and that I had used a big word, mischievous, and more importantly I had used it correctly. Mom was as incorrigible as I was. They now relocated my luxurious living quarters to directly in front of the nurse's station! My fellow inmates, at least the ones who had some cognition, thought this was the most hilarious thing that had ever happened at Hartwyck. This made for great discussion at the Connect Four game table. I was their hero.

5

How the World Views the Disabled

November 2005

The staff at Hartwyck had to train my family about managing the wheelchair outside. So we went on a field trip. We went to one of my favorite stores, Nordstrom. I could feel all the eyes on me as I was wheeled around. My God, this is what my life was going to be like from now on. I could barely speak; I couldn't concentrate on an activity that I used to live for: shopping. All I could see and feel were all the eyes on me, evaluating me, wondering what happened to me, pitying me. I wanted to die.

Then the recreation therapist who was on the trip made the mistake of telling my mother and my boyfriend that I would need a wheelchair for the rest of my life. My mother asked her under what authority she made that statement. She started backpedaling. This was hardly the time to make that announcement, in the middle of Nordstrom, when it was obvious, or should have been, that I was absolutely shell shocked at the first experience in the outside world post-injury. My mother told her she was not qualified to say that and that unless she got a medical degree, she'd better never say it again. I was too overwhelmed at this point to fully absorb this. I was numb.

Then the same therapist wanted to take me bowling with the other patients. My mother refused. She did not want me taken out in a van and to a bowling alley to bowl when I couldn't stand, throw, or do anything remotely resembling bowling. This seemed like an absurd idea. I agreed. My family started taking me out to the mall, to the pizza parlor, and to the nail salon. My life took on some semblance of normalcy. The nursing staff was a bit shocked when I returned from my first big trip out with my family. I went to the tanning salon! The valley girl was back! My sister-in-law Lisa and my mom loaded me into the tanning bed and let it rip for a few minutes. It felt great. The girl behind the counter was in shock at the sight of this crew half carrying me into the tanning salon as I shook like a leaf from my ataxia. My mom calmly explained that I was recovering from a brain injury and I used to love to do this. She took full responsibility for our craziness. When the nurse saw my tan lines that night she was incredulous, "Did you go tanning?" she asked. I said yes and it was great. The nurse complained but my doctor, Dr. McCagg, who is totally cool, didn't get on our case. I came back in one piece, and in good spirits. There is something to be said for that.

My grandmother came to visit from Florida. She helped me walk too. She held my arm as I walked around Hartwyck's parking lot. I could now walk about four minutes with support on both arms; I had my wheelchair at the end of the designated distance. I would collapse into it when finished. The fatigue from this injury is hard to describe. Everything takes such effort. It takes so much concentration to get your brain to work again, and to make atrophied muscles work again. Imagine, Grandma could walk better than I could. We did some serious bonding during this time. We used to fight, but not anymore.

I know that Grandma was heartsick about my condition. She wasn't the only one. As if these early adult years aren't confusing enough, my injury has exaggerated the chaos. Now at the age of twenty, I have to answer questions about why I shake, why I walk weird, and why I can't drive. I do still curse however; some things don't change. The most obnoxious question I have had to answer is to whether or not I was wearing a helmet when my accident occurred. My response to this is that I would have been dead ten times over had I not been wearing a helmet. Another critic told me I should have learned how to fall! If a 1,600-pound animal who can run thirty-five miles an hour and is largely composed of muscle and bone wants you off his back, you are going off, I don't care how smart you are, how rich you are, how pedigreed your horse is, how well you fall, or anything else. There are some things in life we cannot control. It is folly to think that we mere mortals can control everything.

I had to get completely out of diapers before I could go home. Potty training at the age of twenty! My attention span was not good; it was difficult to force myself to think about when I wanted to go and plan accordingly. I desperately wanted out of this hospital though, so I focused, and the staff focused, and my family focused. Eventually, I regained the ability to handle this aspect of living. This was huge.

While still an inpatient at Hartwyck, I finally got my feeding tube removed. The tube had a rubber balloon attached to it that stayed inside your intestines to keep the tube in place. The doctor yanked the balloon out through the small hole in my stomach. It hurt like hell. They did not give me any pain medication. I think the doctor thought that if you were as injured as I was you did not realize that you were in pain. He was wrong. I could now swallow soft foods and thickened liquids. The alien-looking appendage was gone. The doctor said there would be a scar. I didn't mind; at least the tube was gone. This was a momentous day

Mom would come during the day to Hartwyck and Dad came every night to feed me dinner, as I could not feed myself. He helped ease the pain of the long hours after all the rehabilitation had ceased for the day. Sean and Lisa came as often as they could, about five days a week. My stepparents came as often as they could. There were other patients there whose parents came daily too. There were patients who were minimally conscious, and had been so for years. A few patients had very few visitors. The staff took very good care of them, family visits or not.

I feel it was my calling to tell my story so that other young women who are struggling to be physically perfect may hear how empty this pursuit can be. I also hope to inspire others who may be facing tragedy, or horrific circumstances in their lives. I had my brains rearranged like a tipped-over file cabinet. I had to fight to gradually put them back into some kind of order. I had to prove the well-intentioned naysayers wrong. I had to do the impossible.

Nov 20, 2005

I can't stand watching this poor kid put jelly on his French toast! I am sure he did not do that before the brain injury. He probably thinks he is putting it on regular toast. Breakfast in this place is an experience. Actually it is the best meal some of the time; the only problem is that you end up wearing a lot of it because none of us have any coordination. My family stopped asking what I had for breakfast. They read the menu on my shirt.

November 25, 2005: Sean and Lisa's Wedding

Well, this was to be a momentous day from many different angles. Sean and Lisa were getting married and I was spending my first night at home in four months. I could walk a bit with a lot of support, and I was aware enough to socialize. We had hired an aide to help me, but she wasn't prepared for how debilitated I was. My family had to help a lot. Everyone was concerned about how I would get up the three stairs in front of my house. Sean, mom, and my step father Tom stood there as I approached the stairs; Mom had one arm Sean had the other. Sean placed my left arm on the railing of the step, and mom held the right arm.

She said, "Go" in a loud, firm voice. I went up the three stairs! You don't argue with Mom when she uses that voice. Everyone was overjoyed. I could handle the stairs. I collapsed into the chair that they hurriedly had to get for me after this Herculean feat. I was so exhausted from the effort. There were stairs in the house too. Tom got in front of me and Sean or Mom stayed behind me. They made sure I got up the stairs in one piece. I had overcome the biggest hurdle to coming home.

I made it to the wedding in my wheelchair. The beautiful red dress that we bought before the accident still fit. Lisa was the most beautiful bride I have ever seen. They looked so happy.

HEAVEN EXISTS

It was Sean and Lisa's day, but I got a standing ovation as I was wheeled into the ballroom after the ceremony. All these people had prayed for me for months; they did not know what to expect. They appeared to be happy that I looked as good as I did. I wasn't comatose anymore; I had reentered the world of the living. My attendance was proof.

I stayed awake until 11eleven o'clock, and had a great time at the wedding. When I got home I stayed in mom and Tom's room. Tom went to the guest room. This experiment had worked so far.

November 26, 2005

I was utterly miserable on the way back to the hospital. I would not speak. The sadness was unbearable.

6

Going Home

December 14, 2005

I could not stand being in the hospital any longer. They treated me very well there, and they were helping me, but I really wanted to go home. It had been four and a half months since I entered a hospital. I kept telling my family that I wanted to go home and lie on the black couch. The black leather couch is in the den of my house. I used to lie on it all the time. I was starting to doubt that I would ever get out of the hospital. I was surrounded by young people who had been in the hospital rehabilitation unit for years. I was convinced that I would be one of them.

My mom decided it was time to go. She was concerned about my developing despair. I was the most improved patient on the floor. I was starting to realize that some of these other patients were not really getting better. It was a sad and terrifying revelation. The staff arranged for a big meeting. They tried to talk my family out of taking me home; they felt that I would only return to the hospital when my family saw how hard it would be to handle me at home. They argued that I would make more improvement at the hospital.

One staff member, however, agreed with Mom. She said she thought I could handle the outpatient rehab. Outpatient is three days a week instead of the five days a week for inpatient, but it is a longer day. My family assured them that I would continue to do occupational therapy and physical therapy at home. They had signed me up for the gym with a personal trainer. My mom remained adamant. I was going home.

Sean, my father, and my mom came to get me. They were having a discussion about something and delaying my departure; I wheeled myself into my room and in a loud voice said, "Let's go." They laughed. We thanked the staff for everything and off we went, into the new unknown.

Mom stopped working and took care of me. I was so glad to be home. I already felt like a normal person again.

December 20, 2005

I started outpatient rehab at Hartwyck. I was scared to death. I had no idea where anything was, or who anyone was. I got lost every time I tried to go to a session. My mom came and made sure I got where I was supposed to be. I don't care how hard it is. I get to go home after I am done for the day. That is all that I care about.

December 25, 2005

Christmas at home: the best present ever. I have my bagel every morning in the sunroom. Simple pleasures—most of us never realize how important they are. I will never take them for granted again. I couldn't open my own gifts today. My right arm and shoulder shook really badly. The little kids at my brother's house stared at me. There was sadness on many faces as they watched me struggle. I have to believe that this will get better in time. I don't want to be the pathetic member of the family.

January 1, 2006

Happy New Year! We hung out at Sean and Lisa's last night. I was able to stand alone briefly. I even had a sip of champagne. It is a happy new year, and next year will be even better.

January 10, 2006

The staff at the outpatient clinic at Hartwyck thinks that I am too cognitively impaired to be here. They want my parents to put me back in inpatient. They refused. My family told the staff that they believe I will rise to the occasion. They know me; they know how I love a challenge. My mom assured the staff that she or a member of my family would escort me to and from my sessions every day until such time as I could negotiate my way there and back independently. I am staying as an outpatient.

January 24, 2006

I turned twenty-one today. If I was down at JMU I would have undoubtedly had a big drinking party. Instead, I went out to dinner with my family. Dinner was great. I do have much to celebrate. I don't have any social life, but I can walk now. I have to focus on my recovery. That is hard enough.

February 2, 2006

At Hartwyck, they tell me I am making a lot of progress. My family tells me too. I am relearning many things. My memory is still not good. Sometimes I feel really stupid. I am not as smart as I used to be. It kills me to have to say that. It is very strange to know that. Tom takes off some days from work now to take me to rehab. I still need someone there with me. He is an incredible stepfather. I meet him in the great room in between sessions. It helps me to have someone there for me.

March 5, 2006

We are making arrangements to go down to James Madison University to see about re-enrolling in the fall. I am beyond excited about it. This trip will give me an opportunity to see my old friends, and to make some kind of plan as to how I may return to a modified schedule.

We went to JMU and met with their disability staff. They were wonderful. An entire group of faculty came to meet us. There were deans and all sorts of people. I know that some of them simply could not believe that a student who had sustained a diffuse axonal injury and had been comatose could possible be in any shape to attend college again. These are smart people. They know what a diffuse axonal injury is. They know about the dismal recovery statistics. The meeting was great. They were so nice to me. They asked questions, and I think they were amazed that I can converse about my injury and could explain what a DAI is.

We arranged an incredible schedule. They are giving an occupational therapy student credit for working with me, and a psychology student credit for mentoring me. I am so excited. My family is arranging for a cleaning lady so that I do not burden my roommates when I return. My mom will stay down at JMU in a hotel for a while until I adjust. I am glad that I am getting household help. I never did like to clean anyway.

I had a great time visiting with my friends. I saw my old

roommates, and I saw the empty room that was supposed to be mine. That was a weird experience. The empty room was a physical manifestation of the hole in my life, the empty space where I used to be. I am like a ghost, the girl they used to know. It felt like entering the room of someone recently deceased: shocking and saddening and empty; like their spirit may still linger. I am alive, but I am not the same girl that used to reside in this room. It is very strange to mourn yourself. I so wanted to be there, to stay, to recapture my life. I couldn't.

I was a little shocked by the random boys coming in and out of the apartment at will. My roommates do not lock their doors. I could see that my mom was not happy about this. She was envisioning me there in the fall. The apartment was also on the second floor. The stairs were concrete. If I fell here it would be another disaster. I can't afford to have any more disasters. I tried to ignore this; I was just so happy to see everyone. A lot of kids came over to see me when they heard that I was there. It was so great! We ordered pizza and some soft drinks. Everyone just talked and laughed. I haven't seen that many kids my age in one place since I got hurt. People could not contain themselves. One of my dear friends, Frankie, said, "You are still you." He had tears in his eyes. This was the best evaluation of my condition that I could ever have hoped for. I had passed the test. I stayed as long as I could, then I got pretty tired. I went back to the hotel. My friends were partying that night. I knew that I could not handle that.

I saw everyone again today. They were a bit hung over. A lot of the social activity with my friends revolves around drinking. It always did. I used to love to drink too. My friends wanted me to party with them, the way we used to. I told them that people already think that I am drunk; my speech is slurred, I laugh too loud, and I am unsteady on my feet. Why waste the money on booze? I don't need to drink!

HEAVEN EXISTS

The visit was a great success overall. I am not sure how I will handle the stairs going up to the apartment. My roommates will not move to a first-floor apartment. I need to sleep a lot to recover from this injury; they don't get a lot of sleep around here. I am a little nervous about all this.

7

Learning How to Learn

Easter 2006 - The Small Things in Life

Last weekend I went down to a park near my house for a walk. All of the sudden I got an urge to run. This was wonderful because that was the first time I can remember that I felt that athletic drive come back to me. It was such a wonderful feeling to be able to push myself athletically again. I couldn't go very far, and my gait was awkward, but I ran. I felt like my right leg had roots holding me to the ground. It was hard as hell. My sister-in-law got tears in her eyes and said, "I never thought you would run again." She told me how far I'd come since her wedding to my brother in November. Their wedding video is bittersweet for me to watch. I get sad seeing that I was in the wheelchair, but at the same time knowing that my brother and Lisa told my mom that I could live with them in their house if I never recovered fully. I have a special place in my heart for them knowing that.

I am so overjoyed with my progress knowing that I was saved for a reason. The fact that I am going to go back to try college again is an absolute dream. Basically, I was granted an amazing recovery and I have to be thankful and keep pushing.

HEAVEN EXISTS

The cognitive rehabilitation at Hartwyck is getting pretty difficult. I have to learn this augmentative technology in order to try school again. I have to regain my reading and writing skills or I will not succeed. My education specialist is great. She has helped me a lot. My father arranged for Travis, an awesome augmentative technology expert from the Cerebral Palsy Association of Middlesex County to come to the house to work with me there as well. She is helping me a lot. She is helping me a lot. Sometimes it is embarrassing, when I can't do something that should be so easy. Sometimes I cry about it. I can see that my specialists get tears in their eyes too. They care about me, and it helps me to know that.

I know that in time I will no longer need that much instruction. As of late, I am taking my life back into my own hands. With that comes a gradual resentment of people always sharing their cautious opinions. Hopefully I'll be done with rehab by the summer. Rehab has been such a huge part of my life the last year and a half that I'm not even sure what I'll do with all of the free time. I travel to rehab by myself now, with a driver, and I stay there all day with no help. That is an improvement.

May 5, 2006

I ran a little today. It felt great. I want my life back. I want to be the girl I was before. I can't wait to go back to JMU and see all of my friends.

June 20, 2006

We took a trip to Cape Cod this week and went on a whale watch. It was awesome. I love my family but I want to go on vacation with my friends again. I take my own showers now. I can dress myself, which should help.

LEARNING HOW TO LEARN

July 2006

My father and mother are fighting about me going back to school. Dad does not think I can handle it. Mom does. She is coming down there with me for the first few weeks; the JFK staff has concerns too. I have to go back. I have to get my life back. My friends will only be there for another year then many of them will graduate. I can't believe I have lost a whole year of my life. They hardly even talk to me online anymore. I don't think my roommates really care that much whether I return or not. I care.

8

Suicide Is Not an Option

August 1, 2006

I don't think I can handle going to JMU. I am not the same as I used to be. I used to be the hot girl from New Jersey, the girl who ran five miles a day and saw all the athletes in the gym. I used to be the girl with the horse. I used to be the really smart girl who didn't have to study much and partied like a rock star. People remember me that way. Part of me thinks I should leave that legacy alone and move on. Now my life consists of rehab, going on the treadmill, and falling asleep from exhaustion by eight o'clock. Not exactly a typical college kid's schedule. I used to have boys calling me off the hook to make plans; not anymore.

August 10, 2006

My parents kept the apartment at JMU. I signed a lease for the year; I can't believe that I am going back to school. I am going to need help down there though. I will have help cleaning the apartment and I have handicapped transportation arranged. There is stuff all over the apartment though. None of us were ever neat. I hope I don't trip on any of it.

HEAVEN EXISTS

August 15, 2006

I am afraid to go back to JMU. I don't think things are going to be the same. My roommates are a little worried about me being there. They say that they are very busy and there will be some nights when no one will be home to be with me. They are worried that they are supposed to take care of me.

The driving school is going to let me take the pre-driver's test! Maybe I will get my license back after all. I will have to take many lessons if I pass the pre-test. I can't take the driving lessons at school. This is a problem.

August 22, 2006

I passed the pre-driver's test! I am going to take driving lessons. I can't take lessons at JMU. This is a problem; I need to drive. Damn this injury.

August 23, 2006

I decided not to go to JMU this semester. I can't handle all this. I have to learn how to drive again, and I don't like the vibes I am getting from some people down there. I am concerned about being a burden to my friends. That will only cause problems for them and for me. I will go in January instead. I don't know how much more of this I can take. Everyone is so happy to be going back to school. I am to be left behind once more. My heart is breaking. I have to go down and get my stuff out of storage and put it in the new apartment for January. My roommates seemed relieved that I am delaying my return to JMU. At least I will see my friends for the weekend.

SUICIDE IS NOT AN OPTION

August 30, 2006: JMU Total Disaster

I will never see JMU again. I want to die. We got my stuff from storage and moved it in so I will have it for January. I had fun with my roommates but they are still in the typical party mode. I cannot party like that anymore. It is bad for my recovery. I decided it was best to return home rather than try another night there. I can't handle the cement stairs, everything is hard, and I need too much help to stay here. I am too disabled to be here. I feel like I want to go to sleep and not wake up. I cannot escape this nightmare. I wish that I could not remember the athletic, lithe girl who used to go to JMU; the smart, beautiful girl that was the object of envy. I do remember her, God help me, I do.

I had to go on anti-depressants. I almost had to go to the psych hospital. The grief is too much to bear. I can never go back to JMU, I can never go back to the life I had pre-injury. I am different now. The only thing I have to hold onto is that now I can take my driving lessons. I can try to get that part of my life back.

September 2006

Driving is hard as hell. I can't believe how hard I have to concentrate. I never realized how much there is to driving. So far I am doing all right. At least I have the driving lessons to hang on to. There is progress in my life. It helps me to accept that I cannot go to JMU this semester.

September 15, 2006

I have overcome the sincere desire to kill myself twice now, once in the hospital, and once after my weekend of revelation at JMU. Grief and pain can be so overwhelming, so unrelenting that suicide seems like the only way out. It isn't the only way out. Therapy, and if necessary, medication can alleviate depression. Changing your life can make a huge difference, embracing the positive things in life can help. You have to rebuke those dark thoughts, delay the action, give yourself time to get help, to heal. If I had succeeded either time, I would not have given myself the chance to recover, physically or mentally. I would have devastated my family. Then there really would have been no way out; no way out of the ultimate tragedy, no way out of the hell I would have caused them, the never ending pain I would have brought upon them. They do not deserve that. I am starting to feel a little better. I just have to keep focusing on my recovery. The more I can recover the more of my life I can get back. Suicide is not an option.

9

Faith

October 23, 2006

Today I went for a driving lesson. The scary thing is that with this injury I was never expected to get back to this point. I always compare myself to what I had prior to this injury. Sometimes the pain of those memories is incapacitating. I shake those thoughts off; I have to. I asked to return to life. Here I am. I guess the one thing tragedy teaches you is perspective. I have learned just to be happy that I am alive, happy that I can walk at all. I've learned to focus on what you can control—yourself; everything else is beyond your control.

Some brain trauma patients can never drive again. I pray that I am not one of them. There are attention and vision issues with brain trauma. The driving training car has dual controls. It is designed for people with problems. It felt so good to be behind the wheel of a car again! We just went around the parking lot and on a side street for a bit. This is scary. I have lessons twice a week for the next several weeks, unless I screw up and they end them early.

I ran into a cute guy at rehab. He lives at Hartwyck, He introduced himself and we chatted for a bit. He has been living at Hartwyck in their dormitory for several months, following his accident. Nice guy, I hope I see him again.

October 24, 2006

The driving teacher wants me to wait a few months and then try driving lessons again. She said that I am getting better, but that I need more time to heal. This injury takes so long to heal. People don't understand. They think I should be fine now. I am not fine.

I think I am going to try to take a course at Monmouth University. My JMU life is over. Most of my friends are going to graduate this May anyway. I love using the Alpha Smart writing device. It helps me to write. It makes me feel better. I keep remembering things from the past. They haunt me. There are things that I need to rectify.

Prior to this injury I was very shallow and obsessed with my looks and the looks of those around me. I was smart, but I had the valley girl mentality about my appearance. I went to a fancy private high school where most of the girls were rich, skinny, and pretty. God help you if you weren't. I never made fun of anyone for their less-than-perfect appearance, but some of my friends did. We were "those popular girls" and we knew it.

I had been chubby in middle school, so I knew the pain of being made fun of for being fat. One time a kid called me a whale. I wanted to die. I cried for days and did not go to school. It is amazing that one insensitive comment from a jerk can really throw you into a tailspin. Another time when I was playing basketball for Red Bank Catholic High School, the best girl's team in the state, I complained that I was tired of running for practice. My father told me that all I ran to was the refrigerator. It felt like he stuck a knife into my heart. Once again, I cried for days. Worse, I did not eat for three days.

FAITH

I think this is when my weird relationship with food began. I started counting every calorie, making note of every fat gram, calculating how many calories I burned and what I was therefore "allowed" to eat. I love to eat, but eating became painful. If I allowed myself to have something like ice cream, I felt guilty for having it. It took all the joy out of it. I joined the Red Bank Catholic High School track team. Their track team was awesome.

I started running cross-country. I joined because I wanted to be skinny. Most track girls are skinny, but some have an eating disorder. I soon lost weight, my legs were really firm, and everyone started telling me that I looked "hot." I got incredible attention from every heterosexual male I encountered. I loved every minute of it. Girls were envious of me. Little did they know, I had to battle with myself over every morsel of food that entered my mouth. I never weighed less than 130 pounds, and I was five feet nine inches tall. I never became a full-blown anorexic; they eventually drink only water, diet soda, and maybe eat some lettuce, fruit—less than five hundred calories a day. Anorexics literally starve themselves to death in some cases. I did, however, become overly conscious of my appearance, and of my caloric intake.

I think there are many girls and women who fall into this category. I was told I was beautiful all the time. Being beautiful is wonderful; in my case however, it had a price tag. I never felt beautiful enough. Inside this now slender body was a little fat kid with an aching heart striving to be good enough. How ironic: I end up slender, I have modeling agencies approaching me about working for them, and I wind up totally physically debilitated. Life is so cruel sometimes.

My head shook so much when I first got hurt I looked like a drug addict. I could not control it. People stared. It is weird to once be stared at because you met the standard of beauty for society, and now to be stared at because you look so disabled. They are very different stares, and they feel very different to encounter. This injury has really changed my perspective. Now I am glad that my head stopped shaking. I have also figured out that the people who stand by you may not be the valley girls, even if they were supposed to be your best friends.

In fact, after this injury the valley girls were nowhere to be found. One of my popular friends came to the hospital, but when I encountered her in a bar a year after the injury when I was still very injured, she literally acted as if she did not know me. The other popular girls were with her. They actually looked, whispered, and laughed. Not one of them so much as said hello to me. It was an eye-opening experience. I had called them months earlier, when I was feeling particularly lonely and asked them if we could all go out. They viewed this as pathetic. They actually called me late one night. They sounded drunk and in a falsetto voice they mimicked what I said when I called them. "Oh please go out with us, Noelle." There was laughter in the background. They did not identify themselves, but the cell phone did. This was a good time for them. I was now the object of their derision. Someone always has to be the object of their derision; that is the only way they feel good about themselves, by convincing themselves they are better than everybody else. The few friends who did stick by me were Ally; my friend from the track team; Kim, my best friend from childhood, the Trotter twins, Katie and Amanda, and Dana, my friend from down the street. I am so grateful that I have some real friends.

This injury and its circumstances have taught me at an early age not to disrespect my brain by excessively drinking or doing drugs. Previously I drank a lot and partied, but now I find myself yearning to do school work again. Before the injury I tolerated schoolwork as a way that I could remain at school with my friends to party. I saw some of my friends actually become addicted to certain drugs; others almost flunked out of school because they were so often hung over. I am lucky that I survived it. It is a wonder that more college kids don't go under. The norm is getting hammered.

Now I struggle to get my brain to work. Many days I cannot remember what day it is. I have to ask my family if I ate breakfast that day or not. There is so much more to life then the typical college age student realizes. I just wish that I could travel around the country and tell college-age students that.

Life is far more difficult and far more important than the next keg party. I understand that I am more serious-minded than the typical student. I am aware that my reality is far more difficult than other young adults can realize or appreciate. I hope one day someone will appreciate me for what I've been through and the wisdom I have gained. As a result of the accident, I am far more emotionally complicated than a typical person my age. I probably scare some young people, bore others, and simply turn off the rest.

The cute guy from rehab came up again today. He introduced himself to me again and asked me my name. I told him that my name is Noelle, and we talked the other day. He had a blank look on his face. He did not remember talking to me the other day. He did not remember one part of our conversation. My therapist told me that some brain injured people cannot imprint new memories. They forget literally everything moments after they experience it. He is going to introduce himself to me every time he sees me. How is he going to live? How is he going to work? How sad is this?

October 11, 2006

I had a total meltdown at the Monmouth University information session. I started shaking and crying and I felt my knees buckle.

Tom had to get me a chair. I couldn't accept that Monmouth was now going to be my new school. I panicked. "I don't know anyone," I cried. "I don't know where anything is." I just couldn't handle it. The grief was just too much to bear.

JMU was really dead, and so was a part of me. I wanted to leave and go home but Tom insisted that I go to the business meeting. I did, and I am glad I did. After the session, I met the dean of the business school. When he went to shake my right hand, I extended my left and told him my right hand didn't work. He asked me about it and why I looked upset. I told him about the coma and how scared I was to change schools. He got a little teary eyed and took my hands. He said that he would personally see to it that I got any assistance that I needed to attend Monmouth. He gave my mom his card. I could tell that he meant it. Monmouth has a great business school. I will have to make the most of this. What else is new?

October 25, 2006

It's very strange how my circumstances have changed. Although I always have had a deep love for my family, I have also always heard that you don't realize it until either you or they arrive at death's door. Unfortunately, I reached death's door early in my life and have learned the importance of family. I can't imagine my life without any member of my family. They have been so good to me.

My mother has been there for me throughout my whole life as well as this injury. My father also has been there for me. It's funny; through hardship and tragedy you learn about a person's loyalty. I can distinctly remember when my father's mother moved down here after her stroke and he went to see her everyday. He made her last days on earth good days despite her illness.

My faith has intensified as a result of this injury. I actually encountered heaven. It is no longer just an abstract concept that you learn about in religion class. It is real. If heaven is real then the rest of it must be real too. People really do go there after they die. You really do encounter the saints when you die. Death really need not be feared. It is a peaceful and beautiful experience once it starts to happen. There is an afterlife.

I had never really examined my faith until I began to awaken from the coma. Mostly I was going through the motions of my religion. The experience that I had when I approached heaven and met Uncle Joe changed my life. After I had been released from the hospital I began to question my experience. I began to wonder, "Did I make that up?" Upon talking to professionals who understand brain injury and had been aware of my vision I was told that I was far too impaired to make something like that up. I wish the non-believers could have a similar experience so they would know. Some people believe on faith alone; I was not one of them before to my accident. I now know that heaven exists because I was there. Heaven exists; therefore, God exists. I never doubted that God existed, but I was skeptical about heaven and hell and some of the other teachings of my religion. The fact that it was Uncle Joe who greeted me was an indicator that what happened was real. He was dead; he spoke to me about his brother, my father. I did in fact start to get better, as Joe had promised me, right after this occurred. I was not expected to. These facts make me believe that God has a plan for me or I wouldn't have lived. With that knowledge I feel I can proceed on my journey and the Man upstairs will direct me. I say that with as much confidence as I can muster.

Prior to this injury I felt as though I had a definite plan as to where my life was going. In hindsight I realize that there is a lot more to life than what I previously believed or experienced. I need to switch my focus from partying and the Playboy-looking young men to more meaningful pursuits and relationships. This injury, has forced me to mature rapidly and early, I am a bit of a freak.

My perception of time has also changed. I used to be in a big hurry all the time; a hurry to go to the gym, to class, to the barn, to see my friends, always rushing to go somewhere. Now I have no choice but to pace myself. I cherish the warmth of the sun on my face and the wind against my skin. If I get outside for a while, it is a good day. Although the four and a half months I spent in the hospital seemed like a never-ending purgatory, I now focus on it to remind myself how far I've come. I am so fortunate that I can talk and laugh and enjoy life again; the rest will just come.

It is a gift to be able to continue in my life relatively normally. I know what I almost was: a vegetative person, incapable of interacting in any meaningful way. I look at the pictures of me while I was in the coma, and I am reminded of how just how lucky I am. I get upset that I have to wait a few months before I can drive again, but then to think that I could have wound up in a nursing home at the age of twenty helps me to put things back in prospective.

For many brain-injured people, driving again is never a possibility. For me, as well as many others with this injury, the double vision was for a time a huge obstacle. Brain injury is a bear; it can affect everything. Double vision is very difficult to deal with. For a great number of people with this injury, driving again is never an option simply because of their ocular distortion. My eyes have continued to get better and I have been told that someday I will drive. I have been told a countless number of times that a year and a few months are early in this recovery. I guess I just have to keep pushing on and see what comes my way.

October 26, 2006

The driving instructor does not feel that I am ready to drive yet. She says that I need to have a better attention span. I am disappointed, but I knew that I was having a hard time the last two times that we went out driving. We were on a highway and it was pretty stressful. I only can hope and pray that I will be ready in the spring when I have had more time to recover. I can't imagine my life if I cannot drive. I will never be free.

October 27, 2006

Today I am planning on getting acupuncture. I was the biggest critic of homeopathic medicine until I took part in it. We were desperate to find some sort of remedy to increase the functionality of my right arm. This recovery has been a mixture of hope and desperation. I am very hopeful for a full recovery but the desperation now is my social life. There is a fine balance between developing a social life for oneself as well as protecting yourself against the social evils of today.

It is very difficult for me to face that my social life is now far different from what it was. I still remain in contact with my old friends but I recognize that I face a great many consequences if I take part in the same type of social activities as they still do. I am very fearful that I will become "that girl" who acts like a fifty-year-old inside a twenty-one-year-old's body. Although it sounds silly, I find myself thinking that it may have been far easier if I had passed away. You are in absolutely desperate straits if you are considering this. I am saved from these desperate, hopeless thoughts by considering the effect that my death would have on my family. I can't do that to my family after all they have done to help me. That thought is when I realize that committing suicide is a rather cowardly and selfish act.

I undoubtedly struggle day in and day out with the simple things that people take for granted. People ask ignorant and insensitive questions that sometimes upset me. If you do not know someone personally it perplexes me to think of why you would ask if his or her ataxic right arm is ever going to get better. Some people are too ignorant to realize I fight off tears thinking about my limitations several times a day. I struggle with the gratitude that I feel about being alive, and the sorrow that I feel about my losses. The nurses in my first hospital told me this would be the most difficult period I had ever been through. They weren't exaggerating.

I constantly recite the saying, "If it doesn't kill you, it makes you stronger" in order to keep pushing. I have to think that God has a plan for me, and I am not quite sure what it is but I remain confident in my faith and I will keep searching until it becomes clear.

The acupuncture was cool. It did not hurt. I felt very at peace when the doctor was doing it. The most amazing thing happened after the treatment. My right shoulder was not bouncing up and down like it usually does, and my right arm was not shaking. That was a first. Maybe this stuff will help. Dr. Christiansen also gave me these heavy-duty vitamins to take. She said they are supposed to help neuron growth. I hope she is right.

October 28, 2006

Today I am going over to get cowgirl boots for my Halloween costume. For me this is very ironic because I feel that to have a good time with people my age I have to be in costume to conceal my identity and physical disabilities. Clearly I have some social anxiety as a result of this injury. I believe that social anxiety is a minor problem in the scheme of things.

I really hope that God has a plan for me. I realize that I am worried about my future and I am very anxious to one day have children. I wonder if that will ever happen. I used to just assume that all those things would happen. The stares that I get now from men are different from the ones I got before.

10

Helping Others

October 28, 2006

If I can be half as good of a mom as my mom has been to me, then I have achieved my mission in life.

Today I saw my mother arrange a flight in a panic as her mother was struggling down in Florida. My grandmother told my mom that she felt she was slowly dying.

I have experienced my own near death. This occurrence has left me with a different view on death from most people, certainly most young people who have had no experience with death. Everything in my life has changed as a result. I'm going down to Florida with my mom. I am excited for the chance to get on a plane and be there for a family member in a time of need. In years past, I only went down there to tan, but now that a loved one is sick I feel that there is a greater purpose for all of my life and those around me. One day I will make sense of all of this. Until then I will focus on my recovery and whatever is meant to be will be.

HEAVEN EXISTS

October 29, 2006

Uncle Jimmy met us at the airport. He and my mom had some issues over the years. They did not talk for a while. Things are better now. Uncle Jimmy, Aunt Laura, and my cousin Patrick came to the hospital to see me many times. This experience helped heal their wounds. My mom had called Uncle Jimmy to tell him that she was skeptical Nanny was OK, even though the rehabilitation facility said she was. She told him that Nanny sounded awful, and she repeated what Nanny had said to her about dying. Uncle Jimmy said he would try to arrange to get down there.

Mom wheeled me through the airport up to the Continental Airlines area. Uncle Jimmy walked up to us and said, "I am going to make this journey with you." It was profound. Uncle Jimmy had researched what plane we were to be on and managed to get to the airport in two hours. We were very glad to have him with us. All of us sensed that this was to be an important journey.

October 30, 2006: Florida

Uncle Jimmy and I take our walk every morning. Since I am missing my rehab, I have to make sure that I don't lose any strength or skills. The development where Nanny lives is nice and flat, so I can walk easily. We went to see Nanny yesterday. She was so thin. I must have looked shocked when I saw her. She said to me, "Don't be frightened, I have lost a lot of weight." I tried to smile, but I was frightened, frightened for her; she looked very ill, like someone who is going to die very soon.

Nanny was still sharp as ever, but very weak. She could not get out of her bed. She could not eat. The staff kept bringing her ridiculous stuff to eat, such as barbeque chicken, when she could not even hold her head up and could barely swallow. Prior to our arrival in Florida, Nanny's friends had asked that she be given a soft diet, something that she could eat; nothing happened. Mom asked for it again. They said there had to be a dietician to do an evaluation. Mom told them to get one. Finally, after another ridiculous meal that Nanny could not eat was delivered, Mom contacted the dietician herself. The evaluation indicted that Nanny needed a soft diet. Uncle Jimmy and mom fed Nanny a little ice cream.

Nanny loves squirrels. She has a big watercolor painting of a squirrel in her living room. She always watches them. A squirrel jumped up onto the narrow window ledge right outside Nanny's window. The weird thing is that he stayed there for a long time. He walked back and forth some, but mostly stayed there eating, standing up, crouching down on the ledge, and just hanging out. Nanny was really happy to be able to watch this squirrel. I have never seen a squirrel stay in one place for so long.

Sean arrived today from New Jersey. When the car pulled up to drop him off in front of the rehab facility, Nanny was looking out of her window. She noticed Sean right away. She was so happy to see him. Sean and I stayed by Nanny's side all day. I sat on a rug beside her and held her hand. It was a good day. Despite it all, Uncle Jimmy, Mom, Sean and I had some good times. We went out to dinner, and it felt good to be able to support Nanny together as she went through this ordeal.

It is a little weird to see all the Halloween decorations around while you are dealing with someone who is dying. Life is weird sometimes. The sun still rises no matter what.

October 31, 2006: Halloween

I know Nanny is dying. I am not afraid for her though. I know that dying is not the terrible experience that people think it is. Even if you are dying under difficult conditions, once it starts, you do not feel any pain, and the experience is actually beautiful and peaceful. However, if pain can be avoided before the actual dying process starts, that is important. Nanny is in pain. Uncle Jimmy and Mom keep trying to tell these people that.

Nanny saw her friend Andy today. Andy was Nanny's dear friend in Florida. They saw each other almost every day. Nanny was talking with us when she turned away from us and looked out her window into the beautiful blue sky. She got this big smile on her face and seemed enthralled with something. We all saw this. Finally after a few moments, Nanny said aloud,"OK Andy, I will be with you soon." Nanny turned back toward us as if nothing had happened.

Uncle Jimmy asked aloud, "Who is Andy?" Mom knew who Andy was. Andy had died two years ago. Andy was coming to greet Nanny on her journey to heaven, just as Uncle Joe had greeted me the day that I was dying. I think these spirits are sent so that the person who is dying isn't afraid. I was happy to see that Nanny had a friend ready to assist her on her journey to heaven.

Mom keeps calling Nanny's doctor to ask him to come and see Nanny. He does not call her back. One of the nurses told Mom that she thinks Nanny is dying and needs hospice care. Nanny cannot keep the painkillers down. Mom wants them given to her intravenously, but they won't do that. It is getting pretty tense in this place.

I witnessed my mother take on these high-powered medical professionals when she asked to see Nanny's records. They were incomplete. This place did not have a record of half of Nanny's medical issues. That was it for Mom; Nanny is being moved.

The rehab people are angry about this. Nanny was moved to the hospital across the road. They said she was in terrible shape and recommended hospital-supervised hospice. They said she never should have been in rehab in the first place; she should have been in a hospital. They took good care of her. They gave her pain medicine intravenously and said she had congestive heart failure. Nanny was finally comfortable. I believe that some of the rehab personnel became callous to the fact that this woman was not just another elderly Florida resident, but rather somebody's mother. Emotional intelligence is as important as or more so than scholarly intelligence. These people didn't appear to have much of either.

November 2, 2006

This morning my grandma passed away. I was really relieved that she went quickly and relatively peacefully. This whole experience brought to my attention how misuse of power is a problem in the medical profession. One would wonder why an eighty-year-old woman is left wailing in pain during her final days. One would wonder how on earth this patient would be considered stable. How the rehab personnel could continue to say that she was not in danger of dying. This is so scary. How many other old people are victimized like this?

I saw someone standing right behind Mom this morning in Nanny's bedroom when she came in to see if I was awake. I didn't have my glasses on, but I saw a figure very plainly behind mom. I asked her who was standing behind her. She turned to see for herself, and the figure vanished. I didn't know that Nanny had died at this point. Mom had come in to tell me. I wonder if it was Nanny coming to say good-bye. Strangely, I wasn't frightened at the sight of this figure. Mom got a little nervous when I asked her who was standing behind her. She knows that I tell the truth about everything now. It is part of the injury. I think that there are many things that we do not yet understand. I am not afraid of these things.

I know what it is to die, albeit it briefly. I know that death is part of the cycle of life. I know that it doesn't hurt when it actually starts to happen, and that there is a feeling of peace and joy that overcomes you. I am happy that I was able to be here for my grandma in her final days. My grandma left behind an amazing legacy. I hope that one day I can do the same. To have been fortunate enough to feel the feeble hand of the matriarch of my family grasp on to me to say she would hold on to life until my brother got there was a great privilege indeed. Nanny did hold on until she saw Sean. The human spirit is an amazing thing.

11

The New Reality

November 5, 2006

This morning I got very upset while trying to fasten my bra. There was a time in my life when I never once prepared myself emotionally to get dressed. I find that I am still expecting a lot of myself even though small things in life are no longer easy. I find myself putting on a joyful face and nodding when people ask me how happy I am with my progress. If they only knew that on occasion, I have been so overwhelmed with my inability to do simple things, that I end up in a fetal position on the floor, sobbing. Despair is a powerful emotion. I know I may seem a little like a brat for getting upset about small daily activities but the truth is I never struggled to complete the activities of daily living as they are called in rehab. Everything that I have to do with my hands is hard or impossible now. I am so frightened, and I feel so vulnerable sometimes. What would I do if there was no one to help me? I never had to work a day in my life for the necessities in life; my family provided for me. Rather, I worked because I chose to. My life was in a word, easy. That is no longer the case.

The truth is I continually hear how lucky I am, but unless a person has had it all and had it snatched away no one understands. Yes, I have been fortunate in my life without question, but now there are just painful memories of things that I can no longer easily achieve. My therapists always say, "Right now you can't achieve it, but you never know what you will be able to achieve." My response to this type of optimism is, yes I have come a long way but the tears and frustration that come along with this success ensure that nothing is ever going to be quite the same.

November 10, 2006

I just went for a normally relaxing and joyous activity. I went to get my nails done. Yet again I am haunted by the fact that virtually no part of my life is free from aggravation. Due to my severe ataxia I am like a moving target for my manicurist. I feel as though all eyes are on me as I am trying to hold my right arm still. The most common question from people is, "Do you suffer from Parkinson's?"

This question gets very old. I understand that people are curious and they aren't quite sure what to make of my situation, but I wish they would understand that I am not some rabid animal. I am apparently a spectacle. There is no one who is more anxious than I am to try to figure out the ins and outs of this injury. I am continually haunted by what used to be.

I really had the most unbelievable childhood and young adulthood. Unfortunately, I can never recapture that again. Time marches on, and as hard as I try to catch up, it slips away from me. I feel my body coming back to what it was, but I can never again be reckless with myself and take part in the social drinking aspect that was such a huge part of college. I have heard time and time again that God sometimes works in strange ways. I have no choice but to believe this.

THE NEW REALITY

Someone in the hospital once said to me, "I used to believe in God but I can't understand why he let this happen to me." My response to this was that God intervened and allowed us to live. I have developed a deep appreciation and love of the church and everything it stands for. Once again, that's something I didn't think would happen until I was much older. I do believe that I was spared for a reason, but the reality that no one in my age range can relate to this is a big issue for me. I'm finding myself relating too much with older individuals. Sometimes I am angry about this situation but nothing can change the reality that this did in fact happen to me.

Some people do understand what I've been and are not looking for me to be the party girl of the past. I will be transferring colleges to go to a school that is far closer to my house and my family. I regretfully understand that I need to pick a school with a graduate program so there will be some older students on campus. Due to this injury I am going to continue school as a twenty-two-year-old junior; I have lost two years of my life. I realize there are older kids at my old school but they may be the hardcore partying slackers, and they spell trouble for me. They will not be able to relate to me, nor I to them.

In all actuality I realize that many of my friends from before the accident socialize in ways that I am not critical of, but due to this horrendous injury I can no longer participate in them. I have to socialize in ways that are foreign to me. I find myself relating to my twenty-six-year-old brother who has graduated to a different part of life. He is married and a double-career man. He is a Realtor as well as a preschool teacher for children with autism. He ended up marrying the girl he met on his nineteenth birthday. I consider him one-in-a-million lucky for finding his life partner so young. My brother and I are unbelievably close and he has been my confidant through this whole episode.

As if this recovery isn't difficult enough, I have the social impact as well as all of the physical issues.

It's strange how your mind holds onto traumatic events clearly in times of desperation. I recall becoming aware of where I was and asking for cyanide pills in the hospital. For all I knew I was never getting out of the hospital and was never getting out of the wheelchair. I had a God-awful, foul-looking feeding tube sticking out of my stomach. The nurses poured this disgusting liquid into it to keep me alive. I thought that was there for good too. I felt this horror of being trapped in a body that did not seem at all familiar, being trapped in a nightmare from which there was no waking. There seemed to be only one way out. When the lights went out on August 2, 2005, I had it all. I was twenty years old, an athlete, pretty, popular, and a dean's-list student involved in a serious relationship with a gorgeous young man. When the lights finally came back on two months later I was totally disabled, unable to walk, feed myself, go to the bathroom myself—virtually a prisoner to a new and horrifying reality. I had to ask for help in my efforts to kill myself; I was too disabled to enact the plan! Being a twenty-year-old girl and coming to terms with my condition and my new surroundings was stranger then I can even explain.

November 13, 2006

I recently got very upset in the car with my brother. As much as I understand the significance of this injury, I became angry at the suggestion that I should abandon my plans to visit my friends at school because my mom is grieving the loss of her mother and cannot take me. I understand that my mom has experienced a terrible loss with the passing of her mother. But I so want to go to see my friends at JMU. I finally have a plan for a social activity. I think my selfish side is coming through here. I need to go to JMU another time.

I was originally shooting to go back to school in September. Once I realized the sad reality that I could no longer take part in the common social life that I loved so dearly I have come to a more sensible decision: the school, which I had loved so dearly, is no longer safe for me.

I had an interesting session with one of my psychologists today. She told me that, yes, I have matured beyond my years as a result of this injury and my fight to recover. She also said she thought based on things I had told her that I probably was more mature than most of my peers in the first place. I understand that an absolutely terrible thing has happened to me, but I feel that there are far worse things then being forced to mature rather early in my life. I still fear that I will have trouble finding a mate near my age who fully realizes and appreciates my situation. I just have to have faith that whoever God sends my way will be right.

I am so fearful about returning to school in January. I will go from an intelligent, elegant girl who excelled at school, to the new me: a rather forgetful girl, the girl who walks awkwardly, and the girl who has an aide with her. I can never see myself breezing through life the way I used to. I am a has-been in some respects.

I am so thankful that I have already completed calculus, accounting, and micro- and macroeconomics. Hopefully I will make new friends and will be accepted at my new school. It's very strange how my mind drifts to the numerous people who have been ignorant to what I've been through. I am terrified that new friends will be fearful of my disability. Unfortunately, some people think that I am a freak and incapable of feeling hurt or depressed by their insensitive questions. Hopefully this will all eventually be behind me.

12

Rehab Has Its Good Points

November 15, 2006

Rehab has become a sort of refuge for me during all of this. It is very nice to talk and be in the surroundings of people who are all too familiar with what I am going through. It's a wonderful feeling not to stand out. For too long I was the center of focus and I enjoy returning to reality and realizing that many of my concerns and worries are far too out of reach for my period in life. I am going to go down to my old school to visit. I have had a great amount of animosity regarding this visit. I have to let go for now. The only saving grace is that most of my friends are graduating in May regardless. This is a very sad reality but also helps me to realize that everybody must grow up. Those who choose not to are surrendering themselves and their loved ones to a vast amount of pain. As much as I had always thought I had a well-rounded view of the world, this happened to me and everything changed. I now feel as though I am as sheltered as can be.

HEAVEN EXISTS

November 15, 2006

I just had a wonderful thing happen. For quite a long time I would get vicious when someone contradicted me on something I knew was correct. I now realize that some people with my sort of injury are not even close to the cognitive function that I have regained. I made a distinct effort to just realize this and be thankful that I am not in that category and move on. For me this was a huge gain. In the past I would let my emotions run free and get angry at the person or situation. This ability to feel so much more in control has really allowed me to focus on my recovery. Today I am going to meet with the head of disabilities at my new school. I feel a little bit like a misfit now because I always compare myself to what I was. I have to take some time to grieve the fact that I am no longer totally able-bodied.

November 16, 2006

Today I registered at my new college. It was a day when I shed my first tears of joy. Who could have thought that I would become so happy about my education? The truth is that a person doesn't realize how good they have it until it all gets taken away. I was fortunate only to have it taken away for a short time. Either way it was long enough for me to realize that life is indeed fragile. I will never take what is given to me in life for granted again. I am so thrilled for the opportunity to continue school and to continue this aspect of my life.

November 22, 2006

I recently got back from the most memorable trip to my old school. I had been worried about how I would be treated if I wasn't able to drink and party, but I was pleased to find out that I was wrong. My friends, I realized, were just like all people; they respond positively if you treat your situation with confidence. One of my friends told me that I should drink even if I'm on medicine to get way messed up. My response was, "Why would I need to get way messed up? My whole life is real messed up. I already walk like I'm drunk and I would love to get myself sober." It was such a great experience for me. I was able to see my old friends, have a good time, and be in the same old scene. But now I realize that I love my friends for who they are and that while the drinking scene was one thing we had in common, it was not the only thing. It was a great weekend because I realized that I brought more to the table then a cute girl who could drink like a sailor. My confidence increased greatly with this experience.

My friends were there for me, making sure no one knocked into me, and that I was safe. For me, it was cute to see them in the protective big brother role. It's good for me to know that my friends that I made at school are here for the long haul. My brother said that he was so happy with how it went that he would bring me back one more time before they all graduate.

December 1, 2006

I was speaking to my friend from rehab and he gave me a totally different perspective on a brain injury. He says that in some ways he wished he had something physically wrong with him so that people would understand that he has been greatly affected by his injury. He says that people see his physical appearance and the fact that he can drive and assume that he is "normal." I get annoyed when people assume that I have Parkinson's but I presume it is better than people assuming that nothing has happened to me, and then are shocked when my issues surface.

I find it very strange how the brain truly affects everything. There is not one aspect in your life in which your brain does not play a role. When I was doing rehab the other day, I got really sad because I saw a man from the hospital moaning and squirming in his rollable net bed. To me this was very depressing but then my physical therapist said, "It's only upsetting for you. He has no concept of where he is or how long he's been there." I guess in that sense ignorance is bliss. I was once that moaning person in the net bed. I am glad that I do not remember that.

December 4, 2006

I am getting so excited for Christmas! It seems that I don't need any presents this year! I guess I have learned the true meaning of Christmas! No longer will I be comparing my presents to my friends. I'm just so happy to be alive and not mentally handicapped. It's strange for me to see all the Christmas movies coming out and the street begin to transform as every day another house is decorated with Christmas lights.

I feel like a million dollars. I am sitting outside the hospital rehab center and it is so sunny outside and lovely. To think a year ago I was preparing for Christmas upstairs in my hospital room.

December 6, 2006

A good friend of mine passed away last night of a heroin overdose. He was a beautiful kid who had the potential to be anything he wanted. He had always been that kid who lived life on the edge and always pushed the limits. I wish he could have saved his family all this pain. It's ironic but now he is in a better place. I hope that his family can find comfort in that knowledge. I will have to tell them about heaven. I don't tell everyone about my experience there because they will think it is weird. His family needs to know about heaven, though, so they can find some peace. They need to know that heaven is a real place and that their son is there. He is no longer in pain of any sort. I am sure this is every parent's worst nightmare. I am so terrified for his memorial service. I am going to be an absolute mess. I know how close I came and the fact that he went by his own doing makes me very sad.

I just wish he could have beaten the addiction. I have another friend who is a recovering heroin addict. I have all the respect for him in the world. He goes out to the bars with everyone, takes part in the socialization, but never touches a drop of alcohol. I really respect him for having the strength to abstain from the party scene and pursue his own life and dream regardless of who likes it. It takes absolute strength to abstain based on personal circumstances. Hopefully I will reflect upon what he does if I am ever in a situation in which I need to be strong and abstain. I don't think that people understand that college kids from middle-class families are doing heroin. It is really screwed up.

13

My Debut

December 8, 2006

Last night I attended the holiday party hosted by the Cerebral Palsy Association of Middlesex County. My father is the chairman of the board. The center helped me to learn the augmentative technology that I need to return to school. My dad got involved in this long before I ever got hurt. He never dreamed that I would be a client. Another one of those coincidences that aren't coincidences.

I received the honor of speaking at this function about what has happened to me and how it has affected me. It was amazing to feel my inner strength come through as I was in the spotlight. With everything that has happened with my friend passing away, it was an extremely emotional time for me. I was very pleased that I was able to pull myself together and focus on the task at hand. On the way to the dinner I silently prayed to my deceased friend for guidance. It just made me feel as though I gave him a useful duty to partake in once again. Sean came up to the microphone with me, unsure if I would be able to handle this endeavor. I had my notes with me, printed out in a large, bold font. I looked out at the crowd, of well heeled, high powered people, and the loving faces of my family, and somehow, I felt exhilarated rather than scared. I began to speak, and found that the words came from my heart and soul, not the notes. Sean, soon stepped back, and gave me the full spotlight. I didn't need him! I told the truth about my wish to die when I first emerged, and how difficult the long climb up from the abyss had been. I expressed my belief that I had been saved by God, and shared my experience in heaven. I also expressed my deep appreciation for all the prayers, and efforts that people had made to help me, particularly my family. I received a long and boisterous standing ovation. Grown men were crying. It was an incredible experience, one that I will never forget.

If something good were to come out of this horrendous injury, it would make what I've been through a little bit more bearable. For the longest time I have felt like no good could come of it; after last night I think I may be able to speak to groups or students about what I've been through and what things I wish I had done differently. I would like to make people more aware of traumatic brain injury and disabilities in general. I would like to warn young people about abusing their bodies and their brains.

December 15, 2006

Yesterday at rehab I had a significant experience. I met this guy who was injured at some point in his life. He said to me that people often ask him if he is mad that his life has been so compromised. He told me that he is not mad because this happened to him at a very young age. He says that he doesn't ever remember life as a non-disabled citizen. To speak to someone with such a good outlook on life and such a concrete understanding of what is really important is greatly refreshing.

It was wonderful for me to have contact with someone who

hasn't been as fortunate as I have. It really made me feel silly for being depressed about my situation. I guess it's always true that you don't know how lucky you are until you see someone with a similar injury who is not quite as well off. Sharing experiences with so many different people with the same type of injury is truly therapeutic for me on an emotional level.

December 19, 2006

Today the most incredible thing happened. Two former patients with brain injuries came to visit the hospital. They had both graduated college and accomplished what I want to accomplish. They told me that the sky is the limit and never to lose my motivation. It was so incredible for me to meet students who have been brain injured and still conquered the academic piece. I now see that it is possible to conquer college after a brain injury. Just to meet two success stories makes me so much more enthusiastic about going back to school.

I really think that meeting these two former patients has helped me to get pumped about returning to school. I know my personality and I know all I needed was to see that people can finish college after a brain injury. I now think that I can complete college as they did. I realize that I will be slightly older than many students, but in the grand scheme of things, age is only a number. I have been hearing from older adults that basically any age younger than thirty is about the same.

My personality type of being an overachiever has caused me some stress in reapplying for school. I think that I will be able to push through school, but I don't think I will be able to achieve the same grades as I had previously. I am OK with that reality.

HEAVEN EXISTS

December 22, 2006

I really feel like I am coming back. I just saw my two friends from elementary school and they were so happy to see me and learn that I am not greatly compromised. It's funny how I am so excited to see people who I haven't seen since middle school. Most likely, they weren't sure what to expect. No one expects to see me as intact as I am.

It felt great to be out doing my Christmas shopping like everyone else. It is a refreshing change from last Christmas when I was still using a wheelchair.

New Year's is on the horizon. It is a time for reflection. A ways to go remains but I feel confident that every year is going to be better than the last. This is a great change from me wanting to end my life when I thought there was no hope for getting out of the wheelchair or recovering. People often ask me why getting out of the wheelchair was such a momentous milestone. I tell them that my athleticism has always been very important to me. I was an ocean lifeguard, a basketball player, and most important to me, I was a long-distance runner. The running gave me a sense of freedom, and it had the additional bonus of helping me achieve the weight and body type that I desired. Being wheelchair-bound signified that I could no longer run and therefore feel empowered as I once had. One of the less experienced staff members told me that I would need a wheelchair for the rest of my life. I love proving people wrong.

The only joy of this injury is that you are rewarded for all of the effort that you put in to recover from it. I always felt that if I was able to regain some of the things that I took for granted before, I would conduct myself differently.

Prior to this injury I was never satisfied. I was always an overachiever who sought nothing but the absolute best grades, the prettiest and smallest clothes and the best reputation. I was always concerned with being that good-looking smart girl. I probably would have continued on this track if this injury hadn't happened to me.

I guess that I no longer can even consider the "what ifs" because I am who I am. I have a much greater understanding of who I am as a person. Perhaps even more so, I know who I want to be. In terms of character development, and moral fortitude, I am sure that I have not yet reached the pinnacle of who I seek to be. Perhaps this is a life-long endeavor, injury or not.

December 23, 2006

Last night I went to a college basketball game with my dad. When we arrived at the stadium my father became very upset that they didn't have any handicapped parking near the stadium. This was very strange for me to hear. Here I am a girl who often walks for two hours on the treadmill, listening to my father complain in disgust how far away the handicapped parking was. Once I finally got into the game my father and I were climbing to our seats. Once again I never realized that my balance issues were so apparent. The stadium had many stairs. I could conquer the stairs with the help of a railing but one section of the stairs had no railing. I needed my father's support. This was an upsetting event for me, to watch countless numbers of college students conquer the stairs without a railing, and to know that countless eyes were watching my awkward struggle to do the same.

This disability smacks me in the face sometimes. It is very difficult to accept that I am, for right now, different. I am very anxious for the day that I can go to a sporting event and blend in as everyone else does. I am still hopeful that I will continue to improve until one day I will be a member of population with no physical disabilities.

December 26, 2006

Today at rehab I encountered someone with a frontal lobe injury. The effect of brain injury is related to the area of the brain that was injured. Frontal lobe injuries affect emotion and the ability to handle it and express it appropriately. The person I met today just burst out crying twice while I was speaking with him. He explained to me that this wasn't like him prior to the accident. I came to realize that it was kind of cruel and insensitive of me to ask him what had happened to him. I now realize that it was ignorant of me to ask someone not knowing his or her reaction. Frontal lobe injuries cause emotional changes for the person affected. Outbursts are common, he told me. It was clear that this grown man was embarrassed about his crying and could not control it. It was a sad thing to witness.

I spoke to someone else who told me that they were hoping to be back to normal within six months. I got very offended at this because I've been far over a year into my recovery. I have to be careful not to become bitter because someone else has an injury less severe than mine. Sometimes, people have overly optimistic goals. Maybe that is how you stay sane in the midst of tragedy. I was overly optimistic about going back to JMU in September. There is a fine line between making sure that you have goals, and being overly optimistic. I need to believe there is hope that I will recover. Everyone needs hope I think, no matter what their circumstances; everyone needs to have dreams. Even if the goals may be too optimistic, they still provide you with the impetus to keep bettering yourself.

14

The New Year

December 31, 2006

I just had breakfast with my good friend. It means a great deal to me that she has befriended me. I have become good friends with her since the injury. She has never seen the injury as a defining factor to me and is very down to earth. She also goes to my new school, so I automatically have one friend. She really tries to understand what I'm going through. It's comical comparing stories, because I was always intimidated by her beauty. I come to find out that she felt the same way about me.

We had an interesting conversation over breakfast regarding societal pressure to be thin. Over our egg whites and wheat bread we were discussing how women always feel pressured that they are not thin enough. Even though we both ran in high school, no matter how fit we were we both agreed you can be thinner. Even though we both are educated, intelligent girls and constantly hear that the number on the scale doesn't matter, we both feel our eyes tearing up if the number is too high for our taste. It turns out that this beautiful girl had a traumatic brain injury too. Hers was nowhere near as severe as mine. She never lost consciousness, but she did have some of the short-term memory issues that plague me. I think she is being a friend to me in part because she has a unique understanding and compassion for what I am going through. She is a very nice girl.

December 31, 2006

Tonight is New Year's. As with the beginning of 2006, I feel that 2007 will be even better for me. The year 2005 was kind of a toss up for me. Everything was wonderful up until August 2. On that date my little perfect world as I knew it got turned upside down. Then 2006 was spent in my repetitive schedule of rehab, technology training, and rehab again. I predict that by 2008 I'll be much further along in my recovery. I don't think I will be even close to finished healing until 2010. It's really scary how long this takes.

January 1, 2007

I am so excited to see what this new year brings! I'm going to be starting school at Monmouth University and progressing in my path of life. I am so excited to further progress in my schooling. I realize that not everyone will or has to graduate college, but my will to succeed requires a college education. I never want to find myself not qualified for a job because I failed to pursue my education. The school that I am going to transfer to has an MBA program, and I am thinking that I might as well go for that since I am going to be around the age of grad school students once I finish. I am just so excited to pursue my goals in 2007. I indeed do have a long way to go, but returning to a university is going to be a great step in my recovery.

Monmouth offers summer classes, this is a good thing. I can start that much sooner. I need every advantage possible to graduate before I'm thirty. It's going to be very strange for me when I recognize eighteen-year-old freshmen. I know my whole purpose in the college experience when I was eighteen was far different from my purpose now, when I've almost died and lived to tell about it. I remember thinking adults were just nagging when they always said, "Remember, this for when you're older and can appreciate it more." I was too immature to appreciate the deeper purpose and meaning of their noble words.

January 2, 2007

We are heading back down to Florida to take care of my grandma's estate. In places such as the airport my parents always ask me if I want a wheelchair. People have to understand that your pride is deeply hurt when you accept a wheelchair. Thank goodness I don't need one permanently. I swore to myself that the day I no longer needed a wheelchair I would never sit in one again. It is strange how since this injury my view of certain things changes. Since I've been injured and am now handicapped, I get very angry that people abuse handicapped parking spaces. People need to understand that those who are suffering from a handicap would give anything to undo it. So the very least that people can do is respect the accommodations that are provided for them.

January 5, 2007

I went for a walk this morning around my grandma's development. I was surprised that I talked to three different people, each of whom had seen me in November, and all said how much better I'm walking. It was good for me to hear because neither my family nor I realized the changes from day to day. Thankfully, there are small advances every day. I am just hopeful that I continue to improve so that the next time I come back to my grandma's development a change is evident.

It is a strange point in my life that I am so hopeful the elderly people who knew my grandmother approve of me. I am noticeably insecure since this injury. Previously, I was very secure, even a bit cocky. I used to be thrilled if I looked good and skinny. Now I realize that it doesn't matter how thin or how pretty you are.

I am now at a much more difficult point in life. As much as I hate to admit it, living was much easier before I had this injury. A person never realizes his or her inner strength until faced with a time of tribulations. I have survived one of the most trying situations that anyone could ever face in life.

I am now going to pay much closer attention to the unnecessary risks people take—such as using tanning salons (where I used to go several times a week) —and will try to eliminate things that I know are harmful to my health. I am going to try my best to live fully, healthfully, and happily throughout the rest of my days here on this earth.

January 6, 2007

I am so thrilled with the coming of the New Year. God spared me for a reason. Still, I am very nervous about continuing my college degree. Perhaps I will be able to achieve the degree, but not as easily as I would have before the accident. I am very competitive by nature, and I always compare myself to my brother. I see him in marital bliss at the age of twenty-six, and get slightly jealous. Most likely I won't be ready to spend my life with someone by the age of twenty-six. My mother disagrees with me on that, she says to wait and see what happens. I have been involved with someone from the age of fourteen on. Being single is a new phenomena; it is survivable. I have a great deal to focus on and have no particular time for a relationship.

Once I begin to attend my new college, I will be exposed to a whole new group of people. College kids usually are pretty self-absorbed. I was, I probably still am. It will be an experience to see how I am received. Sometimes I feel as though I should wear a sign on my neck that says DIFFERENT. I sympathize for the people I meet who have no clue what I am battling back from. I might be calmly and routinely offered a beer. I will be forced to decline and be quick to state that I am a has-been at the age of twenty-two. There is something odd about a society in which it is so awkward to decline a drink. Maybe it's my own insecurity about no longer being able to be that hot girl always with a drink in her hand—the identity that I came to love at my old college.

The vitamins and the acupuncture are working. I am a lot more energetic since I started this regime. My arm shakes much less than it used to. Maybe I won't be quite as much of a spectacle at Monmouth. Things are looking up.

January 6, 2007

We were looking through my grandmother's belongings and found old letters from my grandfather meticulously wrapped and kept for sixty years. It was kind of sweet to come across letters like that because obviously there was something to their marriage. Grandpa's alcoholism destroyed him and the marriage. Nanny obviously did love him despite it all; the fact that she kept his letters proves it. They raised a beautiful daughter, and for that I am eternally grateful. They used to talk about each other long after the divorce. I think my grandpa still loved her too. Divorce may end the marriage, but it doesn't end the feelings.

Just seeing the state of my grandma's house makes me terrified that my mother and my father won't ever ask for help if they need it. I would be more than happy and consider it my duty to help my parents and step-parents. After all that they have done for me in the wake of recovering from this terrible injury, I am forever in debt to them.

January 7, 2007

Today we are having a luncheon for my deceased grandmother. It is interesting to hear all of her friends speak of her. It seems as though everyone who knew her is in unison saying she was a brilliant woman. I really hope that my friends would say that I'm intelligent even though my short-term memory has some struggles. I do feel like there's a difference between rote memorization and cognition. I understand what I read and what I hear, but I may not be able to retrieve it on call from memory for a test.

I anticipate struggling with the rote memorization part of college and learning. For this reason, I am going to take a nutrition course. I am very interested in that subject, and I think it will be a good place to start. Since I have always been so finicky about my weight, I have constantly read articles pertaining to fitness and health. In my initial return to school, I am going to focus on courses that are of high interest, and then move on to harder courses. I am hopeful that by the following September I can tackle three courses.

January 7, 2007

We just had the nicest memorial service for my grandmother. Everyone kept saying how she was such a believer in higher education and how she wasn't afraid to make her thoughts and opinions known. Nanny had a hard life, but she never felt sorry for herself. She was a fighter, and a big proponent of social justice. It made me miss her more than ever to hear how well liked she was in her community. Nanny was a legacy. My mind wanders to think what my life is going to be like when my parents are gone. It is very scary for me to imagine that. I really need my family more than ever now. Sometimes I wonder if there will ever be a day when I do not need them.

January 9, 2007

Wow, I just had the most interesting talk with my best friend. I often am too wrapped up in what I want to be and who I want to be. She was telling me how she is so happy that the trend now is to get married when you're around thirty. I need to learn from my best friend. While she says that there is so much she wants to accomplish and she doesn't want to get married any time soon, I on the other hand am obsessed with rushing forward. It is refreshing to hear another prospective. I think I need to realize that life is a winding path and not a plunging cliff.

15

Monmouth University

January 10, 2007

Orientation at Monmouth; this really is happening! I can scarcely believe that I was just at a university, walking around with other students, and meeting professors. I love how all the professors were discussing the future. They gave tips on how to approach and succeed in your future. I was reading the guidelines for being a business major, and I think that I chose the right major. I love the financial industry and my new school is in an excellent location for obtaining employment in the financial field. Monmouth is close to New York, and many financial firms have local offices in Red Bank. It really seems that I have made the right decision for a school. I can see myself going to and succeeding here.

I am so excited about starting my class, and hope it is the start of many. I am so thankful to God as well as my doctors that I am here. Basically, I feel like I have won the lottery! It was so exciting to *walk* into my orientation seminar. My old school was wonderful for a time, but my life is different now. It is not every day you hear of a twenty-year-old in a coma. My mind tolerates things differently now. I think that I was given a second chance at life and I am going to go at it vibrantly and with great enthusiasm.

January 11, 2007

Last night was a huge night for me. I was able to fall asleep peacefully and sleep through the night. For once, my ataxia in my right shoulder didn't keep me from falling asleep. This new vitamin therapy that I'm on is really making a difference. It was just the icing on the cake of the wonderful day I had. My life is gradually being given back to me.

I used to hope for luck, but now I am very confident that you accomplish your dreams with hard work. God has taken care of me and He has a plan for me. I am just so excited for every day now. My next two big goals are tackling my first test of my return to college and also regaining my driver's license.

January 13, 2007

Last night I was able to have an evening that was normal and fun, though featuring an activity a bit different from what I am used to. I went to a cigar bar with my brother, my sister-in-law, and two of their friends. I no longer feel any pressure to drink. I realize that people respond well when you tackle your issue with confidence. After I ordered my lime and tonic, the waiter smiled when he brought it over and said, "Made it special for you." He made me feel great.

Many people don't know quite what to make of my issues. I think that by tackling my disability with confidence, people are much more at ease and can socialize with you for what you are and not because they feel bad for you. It took me a while to learn but I now have come to terms with the fact that I don't want people to associate with me out of guilt, or pity, so therefore I refuse to feel sorry for myself.

January 13, 2007

One of the strangest things about this injury is that your insecurities come back to haunt you. For example, I have always had a tendency to be shallow. All I ever cared about was having the most fashionable clothes in the smallest size. I have always been a snob about having a guy who is diligent and business-minded. As a result of this injury I have had countless dreams about people being upset with me for thinking this way. To me it is almost as if my own mind is punishing me through my dreams. The brain is a fascinating and mysterious organ.

January 14, 2007

There are some things about my life now that I find very relevant to my recent recovery. For example, while I was in church this morning I was very moved by the minister's topic. The minister gave a sermon that involved a man reaching the vestibule of heaven and being granted the opportunity to return to earth. For me, this strikes a nerve because I know that I reached the vestibule of heaven and was permitted to return to life on earth. It is very strange for me to talk about this experience with people because I am always fearful that they think I am exaggerating; or worse, that I am nuts. Believe you me, I greatly wish this had never happened to me. But since it has, I believe it is my mission to share what I've been through and what I have learned .True wealth comes in knowledge and understanding. I seek to share my wealth of knowledge and understanding with people who would benefit from my experiences.

School starts tomorrow. I feel like a freshman getting ready for school, jittery and excited. It is very strange to feel like a freshman because I am so excited about my first day of class, but in reality my freshman year I was excited to live by myself. Now I am excited for the first day of class and really anxious regarding my first test. Since I almost had that all taken away, I am very thankful that tomorrow—the day I've been waiting for—has come. In this recovery, you initially go into a sort of dreamland; you long for things to pick up right where they left off. Once you reach a level of awareness you realize that eventually you will be able to resume a life, but you can never reclaim the past.

January 17, 2007

Yesterday I had the most exciting day in a while. It was my first day taking a class at my new school. I missed the college atmosphere so much. There was something wonderful about blending into a classroom. I felt incredible going to class and fitting in as though nothing has ever happened to me. I had a great and very full day. The athletic mindset came back and I was able to push the last home stretch by taking a driving lesson. I was so pleased to hear that if I continue the way I performed yesterday, I will get my license back in a month or so. I was just so pleased to hear that was even a possibility. Granted there are no guarantees, but to have that suggested to me means that I am clearly making some progress.

I am so pumped about these next few months. God has granted me this opportunity and it is my duty and calling to keep pushing on. Today I was almost comical in my excitement to start on homework. I used to be miserable upon being assigned homework. I am not critical of the crazy college scene, but I am not going to participate in it. I am just so pleased that I am recovered enough to take a college course.

January 17, 2007

Another fantastic day! I hope that I can keep my streak alive by having another great driving lesson. It appears as though I have turned a corner. Now I am on a mission to get my life back. No more endless weeks in rehab. Now I can carry on with relative normality. I still have rehab on Mondays and Fridays, but along with that I attend Monmouth University two days a week.

This is a large leap in my journey towards normality. I remember those never-ending days in the hospital when I wasn't ever sure if I would return home, much less college, or any type of a normal life.

January 18, 2007

These days keep getting better, and it's clear to me that my situation is a true testament for perseverance. As depressed as I was in the hospital I am now a great believer in the human mind and spirit. I just refused to accept the wheelchair and my handicaps. I am still trying to overcome this. My balance gets better every day and I will keep pushing to get my cognitive ability up to what it was before.

In the meantime, I am amazed by the brain's ability to regenerate. When I hear the word regenerate, instantaneously a snake that has shed its skin comes to mind. I sometimes can't believe how far I've come in a year and a half. When I was in the hospital I was completely wheelchair-bound, I had a feeding tube, and was in diapers. I am unconditionally grateful for the fact that I have continued to improve. The hospital staff had told my parents that it was doubtful that I would ever be able to work again or to go to school. They meant well; the statistics for recovery from my injury, DAI, are dismal. Their predictions were valid statistically. Thank God, I am now one of those rare statistics!

January 19, 2007

It is about six a.m. before rehab and I can't sleep. I am just so thrilled about yesterday. I just have to prepare for the fact that at rehab many people aren't as excited about my accelerated recovery as I am. I often hear the negative, cautious approach to my recovery. Of course, this is the therapists' job to be cautious, but it still frustrates me to hear. The staff does not think that I will be able to handle any college course. They want me to drop the course that I signed up for. Joyce, my physical therapist, remains the one exception. She told me to go for it. I am going for it. I have to force my brain to learn. I have to force it to do what it used to be able to do. If I don't force it, it will not happen.

I am sure that I will have to contain my excitement about driving on a highway during my lesson the other day. Many of the therapists thought that was too much to attempt in one day. My response is, yet again, that many of the people at rehab, the therapists and the patients alike, have critical things to say when none of them truly know my personality. I needed their cautious advice at times; for instance, I needed to hear from the therapists that my hope of going to James Madison University in August of 2006 was unrealistic. It would have been a disaster. JMU had developed a great plan for me, they were really wonderful, but the campus is big and hilly, and living the crazy off-campus life would not have worked. I still need too much help to live independently.

January 21, 2007

The nutrition/fitness instructor contacted the disability center about my physical limitations. I guess she got nervous when she saw my ataxia. One of the requirements of this course is a before-and-after fitness test. She was afraid that I might pass out during the endurance test, which is on a treadmill. My Monmouth disability caseworker, told her not to worry. She explained that I go on the treadmill for extended periods of time and that I am quite fit. JFK hospital had confirmed that I should be fine on the treadmill. The

teacher also told me that if I could not perform certain tasks on the fitness test, that she would have to mark down my grade. How absurd; picture telling the paralyzed kid that they will be marked off for not being able to run! I don't think so. We will have to discuss this further. This professor probably has never encountered a brain injured student in her fitness class before. This will be an experience for all concerned!

January 20, 2007

Last night I had a moment of deep reflection. I was food shopping with my dad, and I was deeply moved by the fact that I can now walk into the store ahead of him. I remember all too clearly when I could not walk without some sort of assistive device. It is a wonderful feeling to be able to go unassisted into a store. I realize how close I came to never being able to do that again. If there is one thing I could tell people, it would be never to take life and all of its freedoms for granted. I saw all too clearly that it can be taken away in the flash of an eye.

January 21, 2007

I just had a fantastic shopping session with my sister-in-law. I'm not going to lie; shopping has always been and always will be one of my favorite pastimes. Due to this injury, I appreciate different parts of my shopping experience. For instance, it was a huge deal to me that I was able to stand on one foot while trying on my jeans. It was also huge to me that I was able to get dressed into each different article of clothing all by myself. Probably the biggest feat was signing my name on the credit card receipt.

As a result of severe ataxia I am unable to write with my right hand. I have trained myself to write with my left hand. My signature is not pretty, but I can at least sign something if I need to. As a result of this learned skill I am not reliant or dependent on anyone when I shop. I have to continue to develop my left hand. It felt great to have a pretty normal shopping day.

January 24, 2007

Wow! Today is a big deal for me. Today I turn twenty-two years old. Every birthday since this injury carries a great deal of significance for me. I feel like ordinarily, twenty-two isn't any more significant than twenty-one. But since I have returned to school and am learning how to drive again, every birthday is the start of the rest of my life. I am young, and I am going to ensure that I live each day since my injury to the fullest. There is a great deal that I want to accomplish, and I seek to take full advantage of each and every day to try and do so.

My compromised ability to be independent is frightening. I don't know that I will ever be able to live independently. My mother says that I may be old fashioned and live at home until I get engaged. I have considered this, but I don't want to be completely dependent on someone else. This experience has indeed changed me.

I am so happy to be ambulatory and mobile that I strongly object to sitting in a wheelchair ever again. My parents have done a great deal for me, but I am still a twenty-two-year-old living at home. For someone who was entirely independent when she was down at her old school, this is a dramatically different approach to college life. Now I am happily anticipating the academic piece of school. The social aspects of college have really diminished. Since I have no choice in the matter, and this life-changing injury did happen to me, it is best to try to move on.

January 26, 2007

Last night I watched a very moving film. The movie was *The Awakening.*" The story was about people who had a loss of brain function, and then gradually gained it back. My father kept asking me if I was OK watching it. I told him over and over that I was indeed OK. Some parts were difficult for me to watch, but I realized that it was in fact difficult for him to watch. My family has suffered with me throughout this ordeal. I long to be treated normally and I feel that my father now knows that I enjoy being emotionally stimulated, even if it is difficult to watch. The part in the movie when Robin Williams says, "He seeks to go outside like everyone else" struck very close to home. I remember sitting in the hospital for months, desperate for my mom to come to take me outside even for a few moments. Those trips out to the parking lot were the highlight of my day.

I love that a movie like that speaks to me. I truly wish that this had never happened to me, but I feel that it has added another dimension to my being.

January 28, 2007

I saw another fantastic movie yesterday: *Dream Girls.* Ever since I got hurt, I notice that entertainment speaks to me more strongly than before. At one point in the movie, one of the singers said, "I am focusing on myself right now. Sometimes there are points in you're life when you can and should focus on yourself." For the first time in a long time I am alone and I feel fine about it. I am going through so many changes right now, that I feel I would be held back by a relationship right now. I absolutely love that I am successfully carrying on for myself.

I always had a boyfriend in the past, and not necessarily for the best reasons. I was fearful of being by myself and I absolutely love that I have overcome this. Yesterday seeing that movie, I felt as if it was talking to me. I am grateful that I have been able to carry on unassisted by all but my family.

January 30, 2007

I am so excited! I just had a driving lesson and was told that if I can keep up the good work I should be able to get my license back in a month or so. I am so unbelievably happy, much more excited than when I was seventeen. Now I have an understanding of what an incredible freedom it is to have a license. I feel strangely that this happened to me, but now I truly value and am so grateful for every gift that I have. Now, I see some girls in their young twenties or their teens and I wish it was socially appropriate for me to run up to them, shake them, explain that I used to be just like them, and talk some sense into them.

There is more to life than being pretty and skinny. Now I am so anxious to get on with my schooling and press on in my passage through life.

The driving instructor told me, "You are like a different person," referring to how I was the last time I tried to drive in the fall. She wanted to know what I was taking; she thought I was on some new medication. I told her I was not on any medication; rather, I was taking vitamins and getting acupuncture. She called my mom to verify. She was so amazed at my improved ability to concentrate. I think these vitamins are working.

February 2, 2007

Yesterday I had the most amazing, breakthrough day. Parts of the requirements for the wellness and fitness class I am taking involve an assessment of my fitness level. This assessment required going on a treadmill, doing sit-ups and other exercises. I did these in front of all of my classmates. I was able to perform the most sit-ups in my entire class. My health was judged as excellent in all areas. I love being able to stand out as the athlete that I always was.

My self-esteem has been on a roller-coaster ride since I got hurt. I am so happy that now I can be in a class once again to further my learning. The professor was worried about me participating in this aspect of the class. She was concerned that I might get lightheaded or something of that nature. I told her not to worry, that I go on the treadmill for one-and-a-half hours frequently. She was thrilled for me when she saw how fit I was. It was awesome. One can be disabled and fit in the larger sense, which is another thing most people cannot fathom. The kids in my class were blown away. I guess being in class with me is an eye-opening experience for them, certainly an oddity.

I think the kids are not so afraid of me now. They don't see me as a total anomaly. It was good for them to realize that you can't put someone in a box just based on appearance. The teacher, who is very fit, told the class that they should approach working out with the same vigor that I do. She told me that I was a good role model for other students. I told them that I am so happy I can move at all, I will never stop. Having a body that works is an incredible gift from God. I think the teacher sees me in a different light now. I love this class, and this professor is turning out to be awesome.

February 2, 2007

On Thursday, I had the most enjoyable day of class. I performed at the highest level in each of my fitness tests. I was answering questions during lecture and for the first time since my injury I really felt at home in the classroom. It's a good thing that I am starting to feel at home since I probably have several years left in college. I am no longer ashamed to be one of the older kids still in school. I am very proud of what I've been through and recovered from.

I understand, as I always have, that there are insensitive people in the world. I just carry on with my everyday routine and I will learn with every rite of passage that I encounter.

February 3, 2007

I know it sounds very incidental, but on Friday night for the first time I was able to take a shower with no shower chair and do my contacts totally independently. My brother would have helped me put the contacts in, but there is something very liberating about not needing any special care. I now know that I can stay over at my brother and sister-in-law's house without being any inconvenience.

I love that I have finally gained enough personal independence to be no trouble to anyone. I feel like I have reached a point in my recovery in which I only have good things to look forward to. Now I am looking forward to every day of class and I greatly look forward to the day I get my license back.

February 5, 2007

Last night I was over my brother's for the Super Bowl. There is something very nice about being somewhere where everyone knows what happened to me and what my experience has been. I was surprised that some of my brother's closest friends are amazed by what I've been through. I loved being able to show how far I've come.

Most of his friends haven't seen me since Sean's wedding. I have definitely come a long way since then. I am sure that they noticed that my speech is much clearer and I am no longer in a wheelchair. I had an incredible moment once I finally came to terms with the fact that my parents did almost lose me on several occasions. I really want to be a parent someday but I am unsure whether I can be strong as mine were through this.

Prior to this accident, I was always pleading for financial support to facilitate me riding. It is ironic how what was once my passion almost took me away from this world and caused my parents so much stress. My mom was never a big fan of me riding. She was concerned that it was too dangerous.

February 6, 2007

I just had a wonderful day at school. Almost as memorable as my day at school was the fantastic conversation I had with my friend. For the first time I encountered someone looking in disbelief when I explained that my lung had collapsed when I was in a coma. It seems as though people have a difficult time believing me when I begin to tell my story. Apparently, it is difficult to believe by looking at me that I had a very near death experience.

Now it seems like it is something incredible to have in your past. The vast numbers of people you meet in your lifetime have never been in a coma or in diapers as an adult. In a very strange way, I am proud of myself. I realize that it took a great deal of strength and determination to get my life back on track.

February 7, 2007

The antidepressant medication has helped me. I am still taking a low dosage, less than "therapeutic", but enough to take the edge off my anxiety. I really love my situation as of now. Sometimes it is difficult that I am twenty-two years old and still dependent on my mom for rides, but at least I am here and can verbalize my wants and needs to her. One never understands the value of language unless it is taken away for a period of time. I remember knowing that I wanted to say something, but the words would not come out. Or they came out all wrong. I had to learn how to speak again. I almost wish that everyone could have had a situation similar to mine to truly understand how much is taken for granted in life.

I am fortunate to gradually battle back to the body I had previously, only now, I will be satisfied. Before this accident, I was never OK with my weight or my size. I was a size four but I used to dream of someday getting down to a size two or a zero. How bizarre—size zero; doesn't that mean nothing? This is what women strive for? Now I understand how ridiculous that was. Now I feel it is a much larger privilege to gain back the ability to drive.

February 11, 2007

I had a fantastic weekend. I went to dinner with my former equestrian trainer on Friday. I was very pleased with how it went. I explained to her how hard it had been to be in the wheelchair. She still knows me so well, so she wasn't surprised by the impact that had on me. I was happy that we were able to have a nice dinner together even though I am obviously done with riding.

On Saturday I accompanied my brother, his wife, and my best friend Chris into Manhattan for *The Phantom of the Opera*. I had a wonderful time at the opera. It is strange how certain things stuck out as outrageous to me about the theater. I absolutely loved *Phantom*, yet the inaccessibility of the venue was rather alarming to me.

I was happy that I had my best friend and my brother to hold on to. I am so acutely aware of the handicap accessibility—or lack of it—provided in many public buildings. It is rather amazing how many public places remain inaccessible to the handicapped.

February 13, 2007

We celebrated Sean's birthday yesterday. We had an Italian dinner and some great cake. It was fun. Sean and Lisa seem so happy. I am glad for them. I hope one day I will have a husband too. I am beginning to think this is not likely to happen.

February 14, 2007

Well today is going to be like any other lonely day in my life. My family is great but I have so little social contact with people my age. I have no Valentine. I look at all these decorations, and all the advertisements on TV for flowers and teddy bears for your Valentine; they make me cry. I feel so empty, so alone, so unworthy. Mom started crying today because she felt my pain so acutely. She told me that there will be someone for me.

Well something good did end up happening today! Dad came through. The doorbell rang and there was a guy delivering a big bouquet of flowers. The flowers were for me! Dad acknowledged that he knew he was not the Valentine I was hoping for, but that he wanted me to know how much I was loved. It helped. I am in a better mood.

February 16, 2007

Yesterday I learned that my driving instructor has tentatively scheduled me to take the road test on March 5. This is a clear indicator that I am getting better. This was never a possibility for me even just a few months ago. It's really amazing how things work out. I was given a second chance at life, and I have been able to run with it.

February 20, 2007

I just had the most wonderful appointment at my hair salon. I went in there to get my hair highlighted after being in the hospital for four-and-a-half months. Needless to say they have noticed a huge change and recovery. I still love a day of glamour. It is especially wonderful that they understand what happened to me and how every day I am battling to return to the person I was.

Truthfully, I would like to return to the body that I had a year and a half ago; only now, I would be satisfied with it. It's clear to me that through this experience I have grown emotionally a great deal. Unfortunately, I understand what it was to be handicapped. Luckily, I continue to improve, but that experience will stay with me for the rest of my life. In a strange way I am almost glad that I got a chance to go through this experience and see how many people treat people with a handicap, especially with their ignorant questions.

Understanding how hard it is to be disabled, from now on I will never allow anyone I am with to gawk at or judge someone with a disability. As I am regaining the shape that I once had, people are beginning to treat me as they had previously. It's both comforting and disheartening. On the inside I am still the girl who was once in a wheelchair, except now people accept me and include me in social events; now people acknowledge me as they pass by.

It now seems so strange to me, so unfair that people are treated disparagingly due to their physical status. Now that I have returned to college, I can't help but thank God that I am no longer wheelchair bound. I truly feel that most people are concerned about a liability and therefore would be reluctant to hire someone with a disability. I have always loved the financial world, but I am not quite sure about how I would fit in, now that I am handicapped. I remember how people used to look right over my head when I was in the wheelchair. They often acted as if I wasn't there. I think that makes it easier for them. It doesn't make it easier for the person in the wheelchair. It makes you feel invisible, not part of society, not worthy of a glance.

I don't know if the driven, successful business atmosphere, and the people who work there, will give a disabled person a chance. I want to continue my finance studies. I want a career in finance. But I don't know if I will be accepted in the world of finance. A professor from my old college once told me, "There are two types of people in the world, the nice and the rich."

Wow! I just spent time with two of my old friends from high school. Between the two of them the change that I noticed was astonishing. They both are paying their own way and off of their parent's payroll. It is very strange but also wonderful to see. I am very proud of both of them. Now it drives the feeling of desire for my future even closer to home. Both of these boys are only one year older than I am, yet they are so much further on their quest for a job in the financial field. I hope that one day I can join these young professionals in their quest for careers.

Unfortunately, this injury put me behind in my journey toward a degree and a career. It seems that both of these guys and me are far beyond the stage of drunken partying. Both of these boys have jobs, which require them to be attentive and quick very early in the morning. From my experience many individuals in their early twenties are not mature enough to buckle down on their careers. I am definitely mature enough to handle the working world, yet I am indeed very nervous about getting my degree. I will have to work far harder then I ever did previously in order to get my degree. I just have to follow my faith and believe that I was saved for a reason.

February 20, 2007

I had a bit of a tough day today. I am absolutely terrified to get into the full swing of my major again. I was a terrific student prior to this injury, a national honor society member, and on the deans list. I am very fearful for the future. My brother always says that he thinks I have a future as a motivational speaker. I am extremely skeptical of unconventional careers. I realize that that is rather narrow-minded of me, but I realize this is who I am. For me to be content with my career it has to be in the financial field.

I need to be content and understand that medical personnel weren't sure if I'd ever progress to walking without assistive devises or not needing a personal aide. I just have to keep reminding myself of this whenever I get discouraged. This injury is very strange; as you become able to cognitively process your new stature in life you begin to assess how your life is progressing and how it theoretically would be progressing had this life-changing injury never happened to you. It is not an easy process, certainly not a painless process.

February 21, 2007

I am really excited today. Yesterday I had a tough day, but I decided to get on the treadmill. I prefer to sweat out my problems and get the endorphins flowing rather than to wallow in self-despair. I really wish that more people would pursue this method. I have watched many people who let their jobs stress them out, and never understand that one of the best methods is to bite the bullet and work out.

In our house we have a used treadmill that was purchased for $200; to me it is worth a million dollars. Many times, the value is found in what you make it. For many people the treadmill is used for hanging clothes, but for me, it is a fantastic tool in relieving stress and has been a tremendous aid in my recovery. I do not think that I would be walking if not for my diligence on the treadmill.

May 22, 2007

Lately, I've noticed my old personality returning. I went to the doctor a few days ago and was horrified at the number that I saw on the scale. I am well aware that muscle weighs more than fat, but even so I was shocked at the outcome.

I am going to try not to let my body image become an obsession as it was previously. I am on the treadmill for an hour and a half to two hours a day. I know that this extraordinary physical effort has helped my recovery. I learned in the fitness class to calculate calories in versus calories out, and to e conscious of body mass index. I am trying to do that. My family is getting a little concerned that I may be reverting to my obsessive ways about food. I eat fresh fruit and vegetables every day, they have helped my recovery. Nutrition is extremely important to brain recovery. I will never again do anything as crazy as take diet pills. After spending four-and-a-half months in the hospital, I refuse to end up back in because I created a heart condition. I will have to practice moderation this time around

I was depressed and flipped out when I was in the wheelchair. I used to eat ice cream about three times a week because I believed that I was never getting out of it and thus it didn't matter what I weighed. Emotional eating can go both ways, neither of which is healthy

HEAVEN EXISTS

June 1, 2007

I just received one of my biggest and most meaningful compliments of my whole life. Today in therapy I met a girl who was twenty-three and was in a car accident. She was commenting to one of the therapists that I seemed to be a very strong girl and she was inspired by me. I felt wonderful to overhear that I was inspiring to someone else.

16

One Thing They Can Fix

June 5, 2007

Well, for the first time in a while, I feel a little depressed and very scared as to what my final recovery will be. I understand that in many ways I am recovering extremely well, but hearing that I may require a corrective surgery to fix my ocular nerve in my eyes makes me nervous. I just hope that it hasn't been noticeable to too many people. Brain injury often affects the ocular nerve, and the brain's ability to control the muscles in the eye. My eye, early post injury, literally rolled around in my head. My family used to cry when they saw this. That stopped early on, but my eye muscles in the right eye are not where they are supposed to be. They are being slowly pulled down, affecting my vision. In order to compensate, I am tilting my head backward. This condition will only worsen if I do not get the surgery.

I am extremely insecure to begin with and the thought that this head tilt in compensation for my eyes was very noticeable to people makes me rather ill.

I am going to go up to New York to see a doctor who specializes in this type of surgery. It makes me very fearful that this eye surgery will not fix the double vision that I've lived with for two years. I just wish that I could relive August 2, 2005, all over again. The decision to go to that horse show has undoubtedly changed my whole life. My life has changed in ways I never considered. I have experienced many firsts in my life as a result of this injury.

I have battled back against this injury with no help or guidance from a boyfriend. I lost him a year after this injury. I am not faulting him; he did the best he could, more so than most would have do. I had just expected always to have a boyfriend. Now I realize that what I'm going through has etched in some very deep and very permanent scars. I think back on how I was able to be a carefree party star. Although I did make some of the best friends one can ever imagine, the life I was leading was could have led to other types of problems.

June 8, 2007

I am on the verge of tears, as I wait for therapy to begin. I cannot really explain the highs and the lows that follow this injury. Dr. Vicci, my optometrist has helped me a lot. He told me that at this point surgery may be the only option to fix my eyes. I trust him, he is a great doctor, but this made me extremely upset. The thought that my brain is not well enough to control my eyes really frightens me. Of course, some things are going incredibly well; for instance, I received a 4.0 grade point average for my first semester. What if this guy screws up the surgery? What if I end up blind too? I don't know how much more of this I can take.

June 9, 2007

Yesterday I checked my academic standing online. It read: Noelle McNeil, Finance Major. Grade Point Average 4.0. I ended up achieving an A in my health/wellness class, which gave me the GPA of 4.0 Since this was the first class that I took at Monmouth, this was the only one they used to calculate my GPA.

I accidentally deleted some of my entries from February 28 on. One date that stands out as particularly important is March 5, 2007. On that date I received my license. I was so happy to be technically able to drive again-until my appointment with my optometrist. Now I will have to wait until my new glasses come in to help correct my vision. I have double vision sometimes, another present from the brain injury. God, does it ever end?

The doctor prescribed a prism for my glasses. He also told me that there is a genius eye surgeon in New York City who may be able to operate on my eyes and get the muscles back where they are supposed to be, which would fix the double vision.

To me it just feels like one more hardship to get over. I am at least happy that my vision can potentially be corrected. The nice thing was that I spoke to my world-famous physician, Dr. McCagg, who has supported me through this whole long stay in the hospital and the outpatient venues. She told me that she has recommended this surgery to hundreds of people with fantastic results. I am a little bit fearful because I am not sure how I will adjust to seeing correctly out of my two eyes. I am so used to being screwed up now, that I am nervous about being normal!

It has been almost two years of constant compensation for my ocular distortion. My doctor told me that the clinical name for my condition is fourth ocular nerve palsy. I immediately reacted in the way that I would have in the fourth grade. Upon hearing the word "palsy" to describe anything on me, I became extremely self-conscious, embarrassed, and a little bit disgusted with myself. "Palsy" was a term we used as kids to mock people who were uncoordinated. This injury is so disruptive to one's whole life that it seems like an understatement to call it an injury. A broken arm is an injury. What I have is not even on the same level. It is difficult to communicate the significance of what has happened to me. *I lost myself.* My life will never be the same and neither will the way that I think about life.

June 10, 2007

An acquaintance of mine since childhood had me on the verge of tears yesterday. She explained that a childhood friend of ours was injured after falling from a horse but that she was not as affected as I was. I took this as kind of an insult. I am now the measuring stick by which people determine how bad a brain injury is—a dubious distinction, I think.

Upon speaking to my parents about it they told me that I should feel proud as to how bad my injury was and that I am battling back from it. I have to stop myself when I begin to feel angry about how other people perceive me. I have to realize that this injury is coming up on two years ago and the way that some people view me as a result of this is rather irrelevant in the grand scheme of things.

June 12, 2007

I had a fantastic "normal" summer venture yesterday. I visited the beach with some childhood friends of mine. There are some things about me now that are not the same as some typical twenty-two-year-old girl. When I first got to the beach, the sun was extremely warm and I burned my feet. I was not quick enough walking to keep from getting burned.

I started getting upset because I was getting burned and I could not move fast enough. I tried to walk faster, but that only made my balance worse. My friends had to hold on to me tightly to get me down to the water's edge quickly. I saw a look of shock on the faces of my friends as they witnessed my struggle. One is supposed to look glamorous at the beach, not awkward. I had the gorgeous bikini on, and the Juicy Couture big sunglasses, but once I started hopping around, I am sure that I did not look glamorous. I panicked and started crying. I hate this disability sometimes.

It's clear that my childhood friends can't handle some things about my injury. It is a little bit strange to think about, but I am not sure if I will ever be "normal" enough to associate with friends and not have them notice what's wrong with me. I have to keep thinking and believing that if they are my true friends then they will see me through some of these hard times.

I was happy that I did something "normal" today. We did make it down to the water's edge, and enjoyed the rest of the day. I went to the beach today with my friends: progress.

June 18, 2007

Yesterday I saw the men who are doing construction on my house. These men haven't seen me in about a year, when they made my bathroom handicapped-accessible. The electrician ran down to my mom and was asking if the girl on the treadmill was the same girl he had seen the last time he did construction on our house. She told him it was. He got choked up and said he couldn't believe it; I was so improved. This gave me a great deal of motivation to keep on pushing forward in my recovery. Now I see an objective opinion that I don't even look like the same girl from last year.

June 20, 2007

The accidental deletion of some of my work left me feeling depressed. I've learned not to wallow in self pity. It isn't productive.

Accidentally deleting something very important can happen to anyone. It happened to me because of the brain injury. I became very upset about this; I cried and stated aloud that I should have died in the accident. I heard myself saying, "I am so screwed up. I'm stupid now."

My augmentative technology teacher was with me when this happened. She became upset for me. My mom did too. I couldn't help it. That is how I felt at that moment. Sometimes I feel that I would be better off dead. Remembering what it was like to be smart, beautiful, young, and able-bodied is occasionally more than I can bear. I wonder whether I will ever be that girl again. I actually experience pain in the center of my chest when I confront those feelings. Is my heart breaking yet again? When people make pictures of a broken heart they show one heart with a jagged line through it; that depiction is wrong. I wish the heart could break only once. Instead I know that it can continually break, one crack after another, and it hurts like hell every time.

June 21, 2007

Well I am extremely happy to report that I was able to get a French manicure this morning. I successfully controlled my right arm well enough for my manicurist to complete the style. When I first expressed what I wanted, a look of sheer terror came over her. I get beyond excited at taking part in an activity that I loved before August 2, 2005.

June 22, 2007

I am at a very difficult place in this recovery. As much as I am happy with how far I've come, I am still not exactly where I want to be. A good friend of mine has mentioned going together on vacation. As much as I would love this I have to respond that as much as I would love to, I am not yet to a point of complete independence. My parents aren't comfortable letting me go away without supervision. I am so tired of having to feel inadequate. I have to keep telling myself that one day I will be able to gracefully put this all behind me. I am not a normal twenty-two-year-old who can go away with friends just yet.

July 2, 2007

Ecstasy, my summer class is completed. Marketing was a required course to graduate with my finance major, so I am at least making progress toward my degree. It is definitely going to take me far longer than the typical college student to graduate, but I have to think of just how far I have come. To think, I have left the feeding tube and the wheelchair behind to strive forward toward a degree that most able-bodied, healthy people don't have. Finance is a tough major. Maybe I am still smart.

I am very proud of the progress I have made and strive to perform nothing but more of the same in the future. I am going to make sure that I never lose sight of where I have come from with regards to this injury. Even now, I feel myself resuming my craziness over my weight, and I promise to try to keep myself from becoming consumed with my rather shallow ideals.

July 3, 2007

Well, I am thrilled because I got an e-mail from my marketing teacher telling me that I received an A. I am overjoyed because I was a little bit concerned about the exam; I had to recall all of the information from my memory. Often with multiple choices I am able to disregard a few answers and narrow it down to one choice.

The multiple choice format provides me with the memory prompts that I need. I have trouble pulling up new information, even after I have studied it for hours.

I am very happy that I currently am maintaining a 4.0 at my new school. In the e-mail my teacher also told me that I received one of the highest grades in the class. That's impressive, since I am relatively confident that no one else is returning from being in a coma or the hospital for four-and-a-half months.

July 10, 2007

Today was a momentous day in my return to normality. Today I drove myself down to get a manicure. Even though I have had my license back since March 5, I haven't yet driven without a parent or guardian in the car. Driving by myself felt so fantastic. By chance, when I was preparing to leave I noticed a young woman whose gait was a little unsteady; she seemed young but walked with a cane. She looked right at me after she had struggled with the door for a few moments and said, "Life sucks sometimes." I was enthralled by this exchange. She knew nothing about my injury or the fact that I was in a wheelchair for eight months. It made me grateful that I am still recovering and that noticeable unsteadiness is something I have left in the past.

July 18, 2007

Well I just had my eye doctor appointment in New York. Two things of interest happened. I found out that, yes, there is a surgery to correct my double vision. The next possible date to perform my corrective surgery is August 2, 2007. Another one of the so-called coincidences: the surgery will be two years to the day after my accident. That date will mark a new beginning for me. I know

ONE THING THEY CAN FIX

I am through the lion's share of the initial recovery process, but I love the progress and can only hope that it will keep coming.

It thrills me that my injury is undetectable to many people. I am going to keep up with my eye exercises to make sure that I don't lose any ground. My mother and my father both accompanied me to the doctor and neither one of them recognized the significance of the date. I liked that for once my memory was better than theirs. That date will forever carry deep significance in my life.

July 20, 2007

Over the weekend I had a serious talk with my brother. I do understand that what I've been through can help me share my wealth of knowledge with others. I am grateful that this injury did not disfigure me. That would have really undermined my confidence. I am thankful that I am able to tell my story, and may one day share it with others. I know there is a deeper meaning to life since my injury. I am going to continue writing down my thoughts, feelings, and emotional status until just after my eye surgery. Then I am going to attempt my story as an example for young and old alike who are assessing their lives' meaning.

July 21, 2007

I had a wonderful night out to dinner with some friends. About halfway though the dinner we somehow got to talking about religion. Somebody mentioned that they often wonder whether or not heaven exists. I felt comfortable enough to share my experience. I told about miraculously seeing Uncle Joe, and how significant it was that I had total recall of that experience. I shared that I went to RBC because of the perception surrounding that high school. I so desperately wanted to be a skinny, attractive girl that I sought to go to the school that yielded that breed of girl. Unfortunately I have had something devastating happen to me and I saw that friendships based on shallow, pretentious meanings tend to scatter during times of distress. I am not bitter toward the girls I associated with in high school; in reality I am in a strange way relieved that I now see true, deep people as more desirable friends. Prior to this injury I was consumed with having the best clothes in the smallest size and having a good-looking, extremely successful man on my arm. Now I see life for what it is; never again am I going to be deceived by a pretty face. From now on there must be substance behind it.

July 24, 2007

It is really wondrous how well my arm works in the pool. I may have difficulty writing or eating with it, but I can swim exactly as I had prior to the injury. This fact makes me very hopeful about my recovery. I love that I can seem completely normal in the pool. People often think I am exaggerating when I speak of my injury. I would never exaggerate; in fact, I wish that I had nothing to write or speak about. I love that I've recovered to the extent (aside from my ataxic right arm) that people have no clue as to what happened. I can only hope that my recovery will continue and restore me to what I was before. Mentally and spiritually I have grown.

July 30, 2007

I am getting excited for my eye surgery. In two days from now I will head into New York to undergo the corrective procedure. I wonder if I will realize how large an effect on my life my double vision has had. I wonder how different the world will look to me once my eyes are fixed. I have compensated for my double vision for about two years now. I have lived with my distorted vision for so long that it has become the norm for me. When I watch TV before bed I expect there to be a double of the picture on the bottom and left-hand side of the screen. I just hope that my surgery goes as planned and that my days of double vision will be behind me. If I lose my vision, I am really up the creek. I have to pray for success.

August 1, 2007

Tomorrow is both my surgery and the two-year anniversary of my injury. I am kind of nervous about this procedure, but I am so happy that the surgery carries a very positive prognosis. My greatest fear is that my surgery will not go as planned and I will have to have it repeated. I am also nervous about going under anesthesia. What if the anesthesia does not work and I slip into a coma? One coma is too much for a lifetime. I hope I will be awake and alert enough tomorrow to write about my experience through this surgery.

August 3, 2007

I am home and recovering from my surgery. It was very strange for me to be back in a hospital and a wheelchair for a day. I started panicking a bit when I got in the chair. I am very happy to be in recovery for my eyes. The doctor says I must wait two weeks until I can start wearing contacts. The double vision is already largely gone! This genius surgeon was actually able to fix my eye. I am going to keep pushing on through this recovery. I am two years into it and have seen some extraordinary gains. I have to expect the improvements will come more gradually, but I have learned how incredible life can be throughout this accident and recovery.

HEAVEN EXISTS

August 8, 2007

Now that I've had a few days to process how far I've come in the last two years, I am honestly so happy with how I've improved. To think I came from a feeding tube and a wheelchair to a fully mobile college student with a 4.0 grade point average. I have learned a great deal about life, its importance, and perspective. I just am hoping that I can share my story with others.

August 18, 2007

My eyes have completely healed and driving is that much easier for me. My love of life and the simple joys such as driving, walking, and seeing clearly will never be taken for granted ever again.

I am getting ready to go back to school. This semester I am going to take three courses. I hope I don't end up regretting that. The JFK staff is advising against it. They are afraid that it will be too much for me. They have my best interests at heart, but I have to try this. Nothing ventured, nothing gained.

September 5, 2007

It felt great to return to Monmouth. The summer was fun, but a bit lonely. My social life is not what it used to be. Everyone is busy with his or her own life. My situation is complicated; young people don't want complications, they want to have fun.

September 15, 2007

I like my classes, but there is a lot of work. I am very busy. Having the books scanned into the machine so that the Kurzweil program can read them to me, is time consuming, but it enables me to study on my own. If I try to read for any length of time, I get double vision. What did people do before this technology? I still need help to go to school. I have books to carry, papers to retrieve, and the Alpha Smart has to go everywhere. I need help taking my tests. I can't read for long, so I still need an aide. At least she is young and pretty so I don't look totally weird.

September 17, 2007

I can't believe that Dr. Simonelli, my philosophy professor wants me to speak to his classes! This is awesome. They are studying life after death; my experience should be of interest. I will get to meet some new people. Maybe when people see me on campus they will say hello to me. I have to make a really good presentation.

September 19, 2007

Mom and I worked on the PowerPoint for Dr. Simonelli's class. It is coming out great. I have to show these kids how I looked in the coma. Then they might understand what I have been through. We will use the video Tom took when I was learning how to walk again.

September 23, 2007

Wow, making this PowerPoint is poignant. Tom had taken videos of me during my recovery. I had forgotten how badly my head used to shake. The video captured that all too well. Only a few months ago, I shook and had to use a walker.

Tom also had video of me in the old horse shows. I couldn't bear to watch those. I walked so effortlessly, smiled so easily, and was this totally carefree college coed in those videos—my former self, the girl who disappeared on August 2, 2005. I asked Tom to turn that video off. He did.

HEAVEN EXISTS

October 3, 2007

I am scheduled to do two presentations for Dr. Simonelli's classes. I hope I don't make a fool out of myself. The PowerPoint is good; I think it will be powerful. Sean thinks I should make a career out of public speaking.

October 13, 2007

The presentation was a success! Once I got in front of the class I wasn't nervous anymore. I just started speaking from my heart. Some kids were crying; all of them clapped loudly when I was done. Dr. Simonelli was so nice to me; he told me that I was an inspiration. One girl asked me to describe again how I felt when I started to die. I told her the truth, that all the pain stops, and that it is very peaceful and beautiful.

When I got home, I received an e-mail from her. She told me that her father had recently been killed in a terrible car crash. He was in the mangled car for a while before they could get him out, and was pronounced dead at the scene. She told me that she slept for the first time in weeks because of what I had shared with the class. She found comfort in knowing that heaven exists, and that death is not something to fear. She was relieved to hear that her father did not suffer in terrible pain as he died. I am so glad that I was able to help her. I'm so glad that she told me her story.

October 29, 2007

Both presentations went really well. I got the same response from the second group of kids—tears and cheers. I loved being in front of the class and presenting. I think I will do this again.

ONE THING THEY CAN FIX

Dr. Simonelli wants to recommend me to the person who books the big speakers for Monmouth. I think I will let him.

December 2007

I can't believe I am still on the dean's list. I had great teachers, they were so nice to me, and I worked very hard. Wow, I actually passed three classes in one semester. Maybe I will eventually graduate.

17

Last Entry, What I Have Learned

August 2, 2008: Three-Year Anniversary and Final Entry

I do love some parts of my life; other parts, not so much. I am now interning for UBS Financial in a satellite office about ten minutes from my house. I drive myself to my internship on Wednesdays, Thursdays, and Fridays. I really am very happy and relieved that I can drive myself to work. I enjoy putting on a suit, and I have met some wonderful people there.

And yet, I have to be truthful and real to myself regarding my limitations. I can no longer be seven hours away from home. I am not sure if I will ever be able to regain the stamina and attention span to undertake a seven-hour trip. A few executives have told me during my internship that a bachelor's degree is no longer sufficient. They've advised me to get graduate degrees to make myself more appealing when it comes time to apply for a job. For me, getting a bachelor's degree is tough enough. I have little to no desire to carry on with my schooling past a bachelor's degree. I suspect that motivational speaking may be my gift. I am very lucky to have retained many skills and I need to embrace those. My mentor at UBS, an extremely successful female broker, told me I should absolutely pursue my interest in public speaking as well as in finance.

I find myself explaining what has happened to me to help people understand some of my reactions to situations. For example, last week I stated that I was very impressed with myself for remembering that I had left my suit jacket in the branch manager's office. People looked at me quizzically. Once again, I had to swallow my pride and tell people that my short-term memory is far better than it has been in the last couple of years, yet it will likely never be fully restored. I have lost several jackets since this injury. I was happy that I remembered my jacket.

I feel slightly out of my element interning in the financial field. I sometimes feel as though I am "that intern with the problems." Everyone there is being incredibly nice to me; they just have never encountered a brain-injured intern before. I am proud that I do feel comfortable enough to talk about the injury with people who inquire. Yet at the same time, I dislike hearing people say, "I am so sorry that you had to go through that." The truth is that no one knows what to say when you tell them something awful; there is no correct response, some things just defy comment. That is my sensitivity coming through. When I reflect on it, I am lucky that there are compassionate people who really are sorry that this happened to me.

The financial advisors and analysts that I have been shadowing in my internship all have pursued numerous licenses in order to get where they are. I am not sure that I will be able to pass those exams. I will have no trouble comprehending material relative to the financial world. Retrieving specific pieces of information immediately, as required in an exam, is where my disability will show itself. My memory issues will make this extremely difficult. I am grateful that UBS took the chance on me and gave me an incredible opportunity. I have so enjoyed it. I have learned a great deal from the people who work there, and they have been very accepting and supportive of me.

I have been very fortunate in gaining the support of the professors at Monmouth University. They have worked with me and tutored me. On some occasions, they even helped me find my car when I could not remember where I parked it! When I had my occasional melt downs from sheer frustration, they comforted me, and encouraged me to continue my education. The faculty there has seen my strong motivation to learn and to obtain my college degree. They have encouraged me to continue in the pursuit of a degree. I attend every class, turn in every assignment on time, and go for tutoring when I need it. I am extremely proud to convey that I am one class away from entering my senior year at Monmouth and that I am on the dean's list.

Monmouth University is a disability-friendly campus. The disability staff is excellent, the professors care about their students. My case is unique in that these professors are not only educating me; they are actually helping me to redevelop my brain. I guess that is the ultimate goal in education—to develop the brains of your students. I still have some time to sort this entire situation out. I will finish my degree and try to fulfill my dream of public speaking.

I know how important it is to try to understand the perspectives of others. For instance, having been in a wheelchair for eight and a half months after the injury, I learned how hurtful it was to have people look over you rather than acknowledge you through a warm smile and a greeting. People don't know how to handle disabled people, because they perceive them to be different—somehow less than human. Even the majority, who are nice people, often just look right over the head of someone in a wheelchair. I think some of them feel so sorry for the person that they can't bear it; others devalue the person and so can't be bothered. Trust me; disabled people bleed red if you cut them. They respond to a warm welcoming smile the same way every other human on the face of the earth does. And their heart breaks when they are ridiculed, ignored, and misunderstood.

As I continue on in my life and my recovery I will continue to share my feelings with all of those who are open to hear it. I will advocate for the disabled, and try to offer hope to those who despair. I am going to liberate myself from the confines of what I cannot do, and embrace the skills that I do have.

In the end, pain and suffering will visit all of us to one degree or another. All any of us can do is to feel the pain, and then let it go; embrace the good things in life and be thankful you are alive enough to feel both the joy and the pain.

What have I learned from this?

God gave us the gifts of faith, hope, and love. Love is the greatest gift of all. It enables people to do the impossible, to continue to hope and to believe, to reach the human soul, and to work miracles in one's life and the lives of others.

Never underestimate the power of prayer. I am convinced that the fervent prayers of thousands of people from all faiths played a part in my recovery.

Things that appear to be merely coincidences often aren't. We need to listen to that spiritual voice deep within us. We need to ask ourselves what the so-called coincidence means. Is it God speaking to us?

The spirit is as important as the medical treatment in recovery. Only 1 percent of the people who sustain a very severe diffuse axonal injury make a significant recovery. Almost no one makes the kind of recovery that I have made. God literally saved me; all the people who prayed for me helped me. I never gave up. I know that the faith that my family had in me, helped me to maintain a positive attitude.

Step outside of yourself; if you are down; look at what other people are going through. No one said life was going to be easy.

Get help if you need it. There is no shame in talking to a counselor, or accepting a medical intervention if it is necessary. It is better to accept help than to be needlessly miserable. Suicide is not an option.

Sometimes I grieve the life I used to have; mostly I rejoice that I have a life at all.

Tragedy can happen to any one of us at any time. What you do with the tragedy determines who you are.

Author's Note

There are thousands of servicemen and women returning from Iraq and other places with traumatic brain injuries. We must as a country step up to the plate and ensure that these heroes get the services that they need. This will require planning, money, and facilities that largely do not exist now. Brain trauma recovery is a complicated and long process. These people will need a team of specialists to assess and assist them in their recovery. They deserve nothing less.

LaVergne, TN USA
04 December 2009
165962LV00001B/91/P